Isn't it amazing how the tiniest of hands can hold your heart? Author Melanie Wayne teaches you in *A Grandparent's Prayer Journal* to stand in the gap for those little souls whom you love. The topics of these scripture-based prayers range from character building to dream building. There are spaces in this journal for birthdates, special occasion dates, notes for forgetful seniors, your grandchild's photo, and a section to enter special prayer requests from parents and grandchildren. The print is large enough to facilitate easy reading. If you were a praying parent, this carries on the legacy of prayer in your family. If you weren't, it is time to change the legacy, beginning with *A Grandparent's Prayer Journal.*

A Grandparent's Prayer Journal

Lifting My Grandchildren to the Throne of Grace

Melanie K. Wayne

Foreword by Fern Nichols of Moms in Touch International

Tate Publishing, LLC.

This book is designed to provide accurate and authoritative information with regard to the subject matter covered. This information is given with the understanding that neither the author nor Tate Publishing, LLC is engaged in rendering legal, professional advice. Since the details of your situation are fact dependent, you should additionally seek the services of a competent professional.

ISBN: 1–5988617–5-1

Dedicated to Tadhg and Niall and all future
promised grandchildren,
for whom these prayers were written;
and to their grandfather, George,
who has always been my earthly source
of love, inspiration, and encouragement.

Table of Contents

Prayers for Events and Holidays

Prayers for Character Development

Prayers for Receipt of God's Gifts

Prayers for a Life that Honors God

Prayers for Facing Daily Challenges

Foreword

Grandparents play an active vital role in the lives of their grandchildren. Whether we are raising our grandchildren or opening our home to their family; whether they live next door, across the country or around the world, we can have a mighty influential life-changing touch through our prayers. As we are all concerned and shudder at the challenges and moral decline that face this generation of children, we must be about unceasingly giving that prayer "touch" like never before. Our grandchildren desperately need our prayers ~ for such a time as this!

What an incredible assignment, privilege, and honor we have through our prayers to invest in the next generation of those we dearly love and adore. Long after we are gone, our prayers will continue to have an impact. The Eternal God who hears and answers prayer has not time or space constraints. I get excited when I think that when I have gone to heaven, my earthly work (prayer) is still going on. Neil Postman states it this way, "Your grandchildren are the living messages we send to a time that we will not see." And what are those messages that we want to send? Our earnest prayer is that they would be worshippers of the Living God, that they fulfill their God given destinies, and that they love Him with all their heart, soul, mind, and strength. We can be assured that future generations will be changed because we prayed. Can you think of any greater legacy to leave your children and grandchildren than your prayers?

That is why I am so excited about this book! It is a book that guides us into Holy Spirit directed prayers, helping us store up blessings for the next generations. Melanie wonderfully captures the heart of a grandparent. As I read through these prayers, it was as if she knew my heart. Her grandmother praying heart deeply touched my grandmother praying heart. The prayers she prayed were the same desires, hopes, and dreams I have for my grandchildren. Many times tears would well up in my eyes as I said, "Yes, Lord, yes. That is my prayer as well."

I love how each prayer focuses on a particular characteristic or topic that connects with the day-to-day experiences of our grandchildren. The prayers are Scripture based, so we can know with confidence that we are praying according to God's will and purposes. Truly, there is no greater way to protect our grandchildren from the daily assaults of the world, the flesh, and the Devil, than through praying God's Word over their lives. You will experience the peace that is promised in Philippines 4:6 as you exchange your fretfulness with prayer.

Let me strongly encourage you to take advantage of the journal opportunities provided. Think how treasured your prayers will be when passed down to your grandchildren. It will be so precious and powerful for them to know that their grandmother/father faithfully prayed for them. I don't think you will ever know the impact!

May I also encourage you to gather with other grandparents to pray using the prayers in this book as a guideline. There is nothing more powerful than united agreement prayer. We do not have to carry heavy burdens alone for our grandchildren. It is a wonderful support group where burdens become lighter, hope is renewed, and faith revived.

I personally meet with a group called "Grandmas In Touch." It is a branch of Moms In Touch International. MITI is where mothers gather together to pray for their children and schools. My four children were prayed for by hundreds of moms as I prayed in a Moms

In Touch group for nineteen years. [You may want to check out the MITI website: www.momsintouch.org].

We purposely "GIT" together and pray for our grandchildren and the schools they attend or will attend. Our schools have such a great influence on their lives, especially in the areas of their peers and the philosophies taught. One of my greatest joys is hearing another grandmother say my grandchild's name in prayer. And what joy our thanksgiving time is when we thank God for all the answers to prayer. I am so grateful for all the GIT groups springing up all over the world. This next generation is getting a "double portion" of prayer as moms and grandmothers are meeting, "pouring out their hearts like water before the face of the Lord, lifting up their hands for the lives of their children (and grandchildren), who faint from hunger at the head of every street." Lamentations 2:19

As you are intentional about daily praying these prayers, it will change your life and the lives of your grandchildren. May you devote yourself to prayer as we are admonished in the Scripture to do. God will give you an expectancy of seeing His supernatural intervention as you discover over and over that your prayers matter!

May the Lord bless you as you love your grandchildren with faith believing prayers. History is changed through prayer.

Fern Nichols

Founder and president of Moms In Touch International. A sought after speaker at conferences and retreats, Fern has also been a repeated guest on Focus on the Family and other radio programs. She and her husband, Rle, have been married for 33 years, have four children and, five grandchildren, and live in Poway, California.

Author's Introduction

While our children were growing up, a circle of mothers met to pray following guidelines developed by the organization *Moms in Touch*. (I think our children secretly referred to us as "Moms in Charge.") This discipline of faithful, committed prayer brought us through many years of crises as well as blessings. Now, having entered our 50's and 60's, this same group, with several more added, are scattered across the country. Each morning these [now] grandmothers continue to pray corporately, for the next generation ~ our grandchildren. This book provides a selection of prayers born from this experience. It is intended to assist other grandparents who seek to instill faith and petition God's blessings for their families.

The prayers are Scripturally based using the following Bible translations: New International Version, Amplified Bible, New Living Translation, New American Standard Version, The Message, and New King James Version. Often the Scripture verses are paraphrased to personalize the prayers. Where there is a direct quote from a Bible version, it has been noted in the reference at the bottom of the prayer.

There is space provided at the end of each prayer. The reader is encouraged to pause and allow the Holy Spirit to direct his thoughts. As the Lord speaks, the new understandings and inspirations can be recorded and dated for future reference. As God's Word goes out from His mouth, He promises that it will not return empty, but will accomplish what He desires and achieve the purpose for which He sent it. These prayers will be alive and personal to each intercessor.

My prayer is that every reader will be connected into the larger prayer circle which surrounds the children of this and every age. May we grandparents arise and cry out in the night, as the watches of the night begin; may we pour out our hearts like water in the presence of the Lord. May we lift up our hands to Him for the lives of our grandchildren. (Lamentations 2: 19) Evening, morning and noon may we cry out in distress, and He will hear our voices.

(Ps. 55: 17)

Melanie Klink Wayne

Opening Prayer

Heavenly Father,

  I am filled with gratitude that You have chosen to bless me with grandchildren. I also recognize the solemn obligation that I have inherited through them. As I dedicate these precious loved ones to you, I dedicate myself to pray for them with constancy and consistency. May I be as Lois, a grandparent filled with sincere and unqualified faith who had absolute trust and confidence in Your power, wisdom, and goodness. May my faith in Jesus be a testimony to my grandchildren. May my testimony touch them in such a way that they will seek a relationship with Jesus for themselves. Help me to give my grandchildren loving, prayerful, and nurturing support on their journey to adulthood. I pray this in Your Son's Name. Amen.

Prayer of Salvation

Heavenly Father,

I thank You for bringing my grandchildren into my life and the life of my family. You have given me a rich treasure, for which I am exceedingly grateful. Of all the things I pray for my grandchildren, there is nothing I desire more for them than a saving relationship with You. I pray that as my grandchildren grow in years, they will confess with their lips that Jesus is Lord and believe in their hearts that You raised Jesus from the dead, and they will be saved. I know from Your Word that when they believe in Jesus' work on the cross as the exchange for their sin, that salvation comes and they are made right with You. May they exclaim the welcoming word to You—"Jesus is our Master, our LORD!" May they embrace, body and soul, Your resurrecting work in their hearts, which mirrors Your raising Jesus from the dead. May they claim: "God has set everything right between Him and me!" I pray that my grandchildren will understand that You so loved them that You gave Your Son's life for them, and that because they believe in Him, they will live forever with You. Amen.

(Romans 10: 9–10; John 3: 16)

Prayers for Grandparents to Nurture

Spending Time

Even the stork in the sky knows her appointed seasons, and the dove, the swift and the thrush observe the time of their migration.

There is a time for everything, a season for every activity under heaven. A time to be born and a time to die. A time to plant and a time to harvest. A time to kill and a time to heal. A time to tear down and a time to rebuild. A time to cry and a time to laugh. A time to grieve and a time to dance. A time to scatter stones and a time to gather stones. A time to embrace and a time to turn away. A time to search and a time to lose. A time to keep and a time to throw away. A time to tear and a time to mend. A time to be quiet and a time to speak up. A time to love and a time to hate. A time for war and a time for peace. You, God, have made everything beautiful for its own time. You have planted eternity in the human heart, but even so, I cannot see the whole scope of Your work from beginning to end.

You made the moon to mark the seasons and the sun that knows when to set. As long as the earth remains, there will be springtime and harvest, cold and heat, winter and summer, day and night. You will bless us with rain at planting time. There will be wonderful harvests and plenty of pastureland for our cattle. Thank You for Your brilliant work of creation.

Father, it wasn't until I was older that I truly noticed the significance of seasons. Now I am slowing down and have time to appreciate the seasons of life, particularly the treasure of grandchildren. I didn't understand how quickly children would grow up when raising my own. I would have taken more time to cherish the seasonal changes of life.

I wish I lived closer to my grandchildren and could see them more frequently. Instead, I will depend on You to arrange opportunities when we can be together. Help me to appreciate every moment . . . the cuddling times, the reading stories times, the stomping in puddles times, the sharing snow cones times, the baking cookies times, the pounding bongos times. I will try to be completely available to them and not miss out on anything. I will try to rest so I can handle all their energy and playfulness. Keep me from being inhibited or self-conscious and let me enjoy their youth. And Lord, when those appointed times happen, give me opportunities to share my faith ~ my passion for Jesus Christ. In Jesus' Name, I pray. Amen.

(Jer. 8: 7; Eccl. 3, 1–8 NLT, 11; Ps. 104: 19; Gen 8: 22; Is. 30: 23)

Father, as I sit quietly before You praying for my grandchildren, is there any word, Scripture, insight, or particular situation related to spending time with my grandchild that You want to bring to my heart? I surrender my thoughts to You and I commit to pray in obedience to what You reveal.

Word:

Date:

Pronouncing Blessing

Heavenly Father, Your Word instructs me that the power of life and death is in the tongue. I learn that though the tongue is a small member of my body, yet it is so powerful that it is difficult to tame. My tongue is a rudder that can steer my life and the lives of my grandchildren. Regretfully, many of the things I say are spoken without thinking of the power those words carry. Help me to recognize that I can bless and bestow good on my grandchildren. My words can encourage them to succeed. I can create an environment where my grandchildren feel loved, safe, and encouraged. I can teach reconciliation instead of anger. I can teach trust rather than fear, peace rather than anxiousness.

The ancient fathers pronounced blessings on children. Jacob received Isaac's blessing, albeit through trickery. Jacob pronounced blessings on all his sons, "giving each the blessing appropriate to him." Joshua blessed Caleb, giving him Hebron as an inheritance. Simeon gave a benediction over Mary and the Child she carried. May I learn from their example. Father, from my grandchildren's earliest days, I ask for opportunities to speak blessing over them. I want to pronounce a blessing each time I am with them, blessings that contain Scripture and some of my loving thoughts toward them. Remind me to tell them that the words I am about to speak over them contain life and health. Help me teach that Your Word contains the power to fulfill just what it says. It will not return void but will accomplish the purpose for which it is sent. May they look forward to and wait for that blessing from my lips. I choose to speak life over my loved ones! I know I have the privilege of making an incredible difference through the words I speak in the resurrection power of Jesus Christ. Bless them, Lord God. In Jesus' Name. Amen.

(Proverbs 4:22; James 3:5; Gen. 27; Gen. 48, 49; Joshua 14:13; Luke 2:3; Isaiah 55:11)

Father, as I sit quietly before You praying for my grandchildren, is there any word, Scripture, insight, or particular situation related to a blessing I can pronounce on my grandchild that You want to bring to my heart? I surrender my thoughts to You and I commit to pray in obedience to what You reveal.

Word:

Date:

Giving Gifts

Dear Lord, I want to give my grandchildren all the things they ask for. When they clamor for toys and games, books and candy, I want to meet those wants. Please give me the wisdom to withhold from indulging my grandchildren with only material gifts. Help me consider their parents' wishes and their actual needs when making my decision to give. Father, when I choose presents for special occasions, help me to choose items that will show them that I know them and value their unique qualities and interests. Father, be my example. You are the giver of all good gifts. Your gifts are better than the purest gold. You give good gifts to those who ask. You give a variety of spiritual gifts to each of your children and teach them to manage them well so that Your generosity can flow through to others. May I also give gifts that have eternal significance, then I will be glorifying You. My generosity to my grandchildren will demonstrate that I am obedient to the Good News of Christ, and then they will break out in thanksgiving to You. Amen.

(Prov. 8: 19; Matt. 7: 11; 2. Cor. 9: 11,13, 1 Peter 4: 10)

Father, as I sit quietly before You praying for my grandchildren, is there any word, Scripture, insight, or particular situation related to giving gifts which concerns my grandchildren that You want to bring to my heart? I surrender my thoughts to You and I commit to pray in obedience to what You reveal.

Word:

Date:

Praising Success

Heavenly Father, You see the "Grandparent's Brag Book" that I carry around, waiting for someone to ask me about my grandchildren. Forgive me for thinking that my grandchildren are a reflection of me or of their parents, rather than a reflection of You and a demonstration of Your grace.

Something wonderful has just happened in my grandchild's life. I am so proud of him, Lord, and I want to praise him in an appropriate way. After an understandable moment of celebration, I pray that my family will accept this honor with humility. Then we will demonstrate that we know Who extends honor.

I know You do honor people. You place people in seats of honor, for all of the earth is Yours, and You have set the world in order. Unending riches, honor, wealth, and justice are Yours to distribute. Some find favor with both You and others, and they will gain a good reputation. Their good deeds will never be forgotten. They will have influence and honor.

May this grandchild be like Solomon who said, "I am like a little child who doesn't know his way around . . . Give me an understanding mind so that I can govern your people well and know the difference between right and wrong. For who by himself is able to govern this great nation of yours?" You were pleased with Solomon's response and You were glad that he asked for wisdom. So You replied, "Because you have asked for wisdom in governing My people and have not asked for a long life or riches for yourself or the death of your enemies—I will give you what you asked for! I will give you a wise and understanding mind such as no one else has ever had or ever will have! And I will also give you what you did not ask for—riches and honor!" I ask for that depth of wisdom for my grandchild(en) as he walks successfully in ways that please You and bring honor to Your Name. Amen.

(1 Sam. 2: 8; 1 Kings 3: 6–13 NLT; Ps. 112: 9; Prov. 8: 18; Prov. 3: 4)

Father, as I sit quietly before You praying for my grandchildren, is there any word, Scripture, insight, or particular situation related to praising success which concerns my grandchildren that You want to bring to my heart? I surrender my thoughts to You and I commit to pray in obedience to what You reveal.

Word:

Date:

Encouraging when Disappointed

Heavenly Father, my grandchild is disappointed because she had an expectation that was not met. From my own life, I know that unmet and unfulfilled expectations often lead to disappointment. My grandchild's disappointment may have originated from not getting some item, not being able to attend some event or party, not winning some honor, not holding on to a relationship. These may not have been bad things to hope for, but Your Word tells her that desires become harmful when they are based on selfish motives.

May my relationship with this grandchild be built on such trust that she feels safe in turning to me in her pain. Help me to guide her to You, her Father, through prayer and conversation. You will need to show her where she misunderstood Your intention. She will need to see that Your nearness, Your Presence, is the chief thing she should seek after and trust in. Give me wisdom to respond to her with godly advice. May I discern what words will comfort her, and what words will lead her to self-discovery. I ask that You keep her from blame placing, from scheming, from slipping into depression, from anger. Instead, enable her to submit herself to You, resist the devil, and the enemy will flee. May she draw near to You in humility and seek Your grace. You will show her where her expectations did not align with Your will. As she gives You access to her heart, You, God will lift her up, transform her motives, and change her expectations. You will withhold from her the things that will harm her in any way. Thank you for this disappointment for it indicates that we can trust You to protect her ways and her life. In Jesus' Name, I pray. Amen.

(James 4: 1–10)

Father, as I sit quietly before You praying for my grandchildren, is there any word, Scripture, insight, or particular situation related to this topic which concerns my grandchildren that You want to bring to my heart? I surrender my thoughts to You and I commit to pray in obedience to what You reveal.

Word:

Date:

Teaching the Bible

Father, Your Word reveals that the commandments of the LORD are right, bringing joy to the heart. The commands of the LORD are clear, giving insight to life. All Your commandments are trustworthy, and those who study Your commandments and reflect on Your ways are even wiser than their elders, for they keep Your commandments. Your commandments give understanding; they expose every false way of life. Those who obey Your commandments are the ones who love You. And because they love You, You will love them, and Jesus will love them, and Jesus will reveal Himself to each one of them. It would be better if people had never known the right way to live than to know it and then reject the holy commandments that were given to them.

As the psalmist wrote, "Your decrees please me; they give me wise advice. Make me walk along the path of your commands, for that is where my happiness is found." My grandchildren have begun their pilgrimage with You. They will delight themselves in Your Word, for in the pages of the Bible they will encounter the Living Word, Jesus. Even as children, they will open Your Word with *Bibles for Toddlers* and flannel board stories. They will memorize simple verses and sing Bible songs. I thank You for every teacher who opens this living document to my grandchildren.

As they grow, make my grandchildren eager students of Your Word. If they will apply themselves to the discipline of study and meditation, they will experience total transformation. You instructed the Israelites to write Your laws on their gates and doorposts. "So commit yourselves completely to these words of Mine. Tie them to your hands as a reminder, and wear them on your forehead." Your purpose was to direct their minds repeatedly toward thoughts of You. Jesus brought change, writing Your laws on our hearts. And though we are no longer under the law, my grandchildren will need to know Your thoughts, Your will, and Your ways. This will come through ingrained habits of study. Help me train my grandchildren to study. They will need repetition in learning Your Word. It will not come through half-hearted effort. They will need the indwelling Holy Spirit in order to comprehend what they study; He opens Truth to their minds. They will need to reflect on and apply what they have learned, for Your Word is living and active. Sharper than any double-edged sword, it penetrates even to dividing soul and spirit, joints and marrow; it judges the thoughts and attitudes of the heart. My grandchildren must also develop the practice of meditation. Bible study and meditation are not single acts. Father, may my grandchildren make these disciplines a way of life. Use me, a grandparent, to teach these disciplines of the faith and to provide opportunities for application. In Your Son's Name, I pray. Amen.

(Ps. 19: 8; Ps. 111:7; Ps. 119: 15, 100; 128,104; John 14: 21;
2 Peter 2: 21; Ps. 119: 24, 35; Deut. 11: 18; Heb. 4: 12)

Father, as I sit quietly before You praying for my grandchildren, is there any word, Scripture, insight, or particular situation related to this topic which concerns my grandchildren that You want to bring to my heart? I surrender my thoughts to You and I commit to pray in obedience to what You reveal.

Word:

Date:

Teaching How to Pray

Father in heaven, what a blessing, joy, and privilege to pray with my grandchildren. From their earliest days, I carried them in my arms and whispered secret prayers while they slept. I rocked them to sleep as toddlers saying, "Now I lay me down to sleep . . ." You are my Teacher in the School of Prayer. Your lessons are so profound and Your teaching so glorious that it will take all of my life under Your tutelage to learn how to pray. Yet, my grandchildren will look to me to observe how I enter into Your Presence. Together we will join hands and bow our hearts to You. Ears to hear and eyes to see—both are gifts from You. Teach them the tender and profound salutation, "My Father." Lead us to worship together in Your Presence. Give them understanding of the indwelling Holy Spirit Who will inspire our prayers. May I demonstrate how to yield in entire surrender, praying with all my heart and strength. Help me open to them what You promise in Your Word so that they can understand and believe what is possible for their lives. Train us to pray believing that we will have what we ask for if we pray according to Your will for our lives. We will start with simple requests. In time and through experience You will fan into flame their desire to abide in You, praying at all times on every occasion in the power of the Holy Spirit. Let faith take possession of my grandchildren's hearts as they learn that there is no life apart from You. As Your disciples requested, "Lord, teach us to pray." Amen.

(Luke 5: 16; Luke 9: 18; Luke 11: 1; Prov. 20: 12; Eph. 6: 18)

Father, as I sit quietly before You praying for my grandchildren, is there any word, Scripture, insight, or particular situation related to this topic on prayer which concerns my grandchildren that You want to bring to my heart? I surrender my thoughts to You and I commit to pray in obedience to what You reveal.

Word:

Date:

Teaching How to Listen

     •

Father, one of the most precious times of my day is when I sit at Your feet and listen to what You speak into my heart. That is the moment when I no longer think my own thoughts, but receive Your divine counsel. You have promised to make Your will known to me by Your Holy Spirit, the Guide into all truth. I want that intimacy for my grandchildren. As I teach my grandchildren to pray, I ask for Your inspiration in showing them how to listen to Your Voice. Their ears will be filled with a clamoring world vying for attention, but You can pierce through those sounds, speak but a word, and their hearts will be stilled.

Give me opportunities to tell my grandchildren such stories as the one of Elijah on the mountain. You passed by and a great and strong wind tore into the mountains and broke the rocks in pieces. But You were not in the wind. And after the wind there was a mighty earthquake, but You were not in the earthquake. And after the earthquake was a consuming fire, but You were not in the fire. And after the fire, there was a still small voice. When Elijah heard it, he wrapped his face in his mantle and went out and stood in the entrance of the cave. Suddenly a voice came to him, and said, "What are you doing here?" You, Lord God, were that quiet, life-transforming Voice.

Father, I pray that my grandchildren will learn from my example and instruction how to seek a stillness of soul. May they learn to wait to be fed by Your Presence. The psalmist wrote, "They soon forgot His works; they waited not for His counsel." I pray my grandchildren will have ears to hear and a desire to know Your counsel. May they have a passion to recognize and follow Your Voice. Teach them to listen and obey Your voice. Your sheep hear Your voice, and You know them, and they follow You. In Jesus' Name, I pray, Amen.

(1 Kings 19: 11–13; Psalm 106: 13 NKJV; Gen 27: 8; John 10: 27)

Father, as I sit quietly before You praying for my grandchildren, is there any word, Scripture, insight, or particular situation related to this topic on listening which concerns my grandchildren that You want to bring to my heart? I surrender my thoughts to You and I commit to pray in obedience to what You reveal.

Word:

Date:

Teaching How to Give of Oneself

Most gracious Father, I am always humbled by the Apostle Paul's self-description, written in his letter to the Romans: "from Paul, a bond servant of Jesus Christ." He was a surrendered man, *doulos (Greek)*, a slave, subjugated to the King. Believers use these words, but our behavior demonstrates what we really believe. It is often the case that we profess that we are surrendered to Jesus, that we are His servants; that we possess a desire to meet the needs of the poor and marginalized; that we believe we should take the Gospel to the lost; that we should sacrificially give time, talent, and money toward building Your Kingdom. But we also live as though You are irrelevant to our lives, and we are here on earth to serve ourselves. Forgive me, Lord; forgive Your people. We are in need of Your mercy.

Father, would You help me to teach my grandchildren that You want their hearts. You desire to see them emptied of self and poured into others. Your Word instructs us in the Book of James that people may argue that some have faith; others have good deeds. James wrote, "I cannot see your faith if you do not have good deeds, but I will show you my faith through my good deeds . . . When will you ever learn that faith which does not result in good deeds is useless? We are made right with God by what we do, not by faith alone. Just as the body is dead without a spirit, so also faith is dead without good deeds."

I pray for opportunities to teach my grandchildren how to demonstrate their faith by putting their hearts and hands to work. Father, would You open to my family experiences in reaching those who do not know You. Perhaps it will be a short term mission trip abroad. It might be building projects or feeding programs in our inner city neighborhoods. We may be invited to work at a homeless shelter or orphanage. I pray for opportunities that will remove my grandchildren from life's distractions so they can encounter You through serving others. I pray for unknown and uncomfortable settings of service so they can taste weakness and dependency. I pray for group outreaches where they will learn to yield their rights and sacrifice their individualism for the good of the team. I pray for cross-cultural experiences so that my grandchildren can learn about Your heart for all peoples and cultures. Get us out of our comfort zone, Lord God. And teach my grandchildren that faith apart from its works of obedience is dead. In Jesus' Name, I pray.

(Romans 1: 1; James 2: 18–26 NLT)

Father, as I sit quietly before You praying for my grandchildren, is there any word, Scripture, insight, or particular situation related to this topic which concerns my grandchildren that You want to bring to my heart? I surrender my thoughts to You and I commit to pray in obedience to what You reveal.

Word:

Date:

Supporting Parents

O Lord, do not let me place myself between my adult children and my grandchildren! I do not know all the facts. I was not there when the incident took place. I will need Your wisdom to affirm their parents in the decisions and choices they are making for their children while offering an understanding ear to hear my grandchildren's frustrations. Keep me from ever undermining my family's leadership and authority. Lord, I am discovering that I am not as rigid as I was when I was younger. My tendency has moved toward permissiveness and indulgence. This does not support my adult children in their role to raise their children with healthy boundaries. May I put aside my own inclinations and embrace my children's decisions in matters of discipline, spending money, establishing rules, and setting family standards. Let me lovingly withhold from my grandchildren if giving in will cause conflict in what is expected of them. I promise to spoil only in the small things, Lord! I will need Your help. Amen.

(Prov. 23: 24; Prov. 22: 6)

Father, as I sit quietly before You praying for my grandchildren, is there any word, Scripture, insight, or particular situation related to this topic which concerns my grandchildren that You want to bring to my heart? I surrender my thoughts to You and I commit to pray in obedience to what You reveal.

Word:

Date:

Offering Advice ~ Sharing Wisdom

Heavenly Father, according to Your Word, "A man will leave his father and mother and be united to his wife, and they will become one flesh." At that time, the couple becomes their own family unit, and we parents are charged with doing all we can to support their marriage. At times, particularly when these adult children are just starting out in life, they will come to me for advice. Father, I want to be the very best parent and in-law, speaking only words of wisdom. I do not want to impose my ways on this new family, nor interfere with their decisions. I have several models in Scripture after which to pattern my behavior ~ Jethro, Moses' father-in-law and Naomi, Ruth's mother-in-law. Moses went to Jethro seeking his advice: "I would like to go back to Egypt to visit my family. I don't even know whether they are still alive." Jethro gave his blessing. Much later, after the exodus from Egypt, Jethro heard about all the wonderful things God had done for Moses and his people, the Israelites. He went to visit him and saw the enormous responsibilities placed on Moses as leader. "You're going to wear yourself out ~ and the people, too. This job is too heavy a burden for you to handle all by yourself. Now let me give you a word of advice." Jethro initiated the plan of appointing judges to lessen the burden of leadership. "They will help you carry the load, making the task easier for you. If you follow this advice, and if God directs you to do so, then you will be able to endure the pressures, and all these people will go home in peace." Moses listened to his father-in-law's advice, followed his suggestions, and the burden was lifted.

Ruth so valued her mother-in-law Naomi that she said, "Don't ask me to leave you and turn back. I will go wherever you go and live wherever you live. Your people will be my people, and your God will be my God. I will die where you die and will be buried there." Naomi led her daughter-in-law to the One True God.

Father, keep me from offering unsolicited advice regarding my grandchildren. I know that when their parents are confused, they will seek You and will act according to Your direction. May I be available when they find it difficult to clearly discern Your Voice or when they need confirmation on their decision. May I be a sounding board, supportive and not divisive. Give me the grace to withhold criticism or correction or "that's the way I did it." I trust my children's walk with You, and I know they will submit their requests to You first before seeking me. This is Your way, Father. Help me to always defer to You. In Jesus' Name. Amen.

(Gen. 2: 24 NIV; Ex. 4: 18; Ex. 18: 17–27 NLT; Ruth 1: 16–17 NLT)

Father, as I sit quietly before You praying for my grandchildren, is there any word, Scripture, insight, or particular situation related to this topic which concerns my grandchildren that You want to bring to my heart? I surrender my thoughts to You and I commit to pray in obedience to what You reveal.

Word:

Date:

Naming a Child

Heavenly Father, I know that a "name" holds a significant value. In ancient cultures a name did more than identify a person. It communicated something of the essence, the character, and the reputation of the person being named. I tried suggesting "Jedidiah" with the first grandson, "Loved by the Lord." What a wonderful name that would be! You know that that particular name didn't go over very well with his parents. Zebulun–honor; Asher–happy; Dan– he has vindicated; Benjamin–son of my right hand; Judah–praise; Eliezer–God is helper; Samuel–heard of God; Sarah–princess; Isaac– he laughs. What wonderful names and meanings. Lord, even though my grandchildren have been given carefully selected names by their parents, Your Word tells me that to him who overcomes, You will give him a white stone with a new name written on it, known only to him who receives it. That is a mystery. As I pray for each of my grandchildren, will You give me clues to the essence and character of these children so that I can see what You see? At one time You revealed to me that one grandchild's spiritual name meant, "There will be no other!" I stand on that promise that nothing will supplant Your place in his life. Another time You said, "He will be like David ~ *"a man after My own heart, for he will do everything I want him to."* May that be so. I will ask You for revelation when praying for these children, and I will record and stand on the meanings You impart to me. I will rejoice that their names are written in heaven. Their names are in the book of life. Thank You that those whose names are written in the Lamb's Book of Life will be allowed into Your Presence. Thank You that all who are victorious will be clothed in white.

You will never erase their names from the Book of Life, but You will announce before all of heaven and Your angels that they belong to Jesus Christ. And Jesus will write Your name on them, and they will be citizens in the city of my God ~ the new Jerusalem that comes down from heaven. They will have Jesus' Name inscribed upon them. You have written their names on the palm of Your hand. Thank You for this wondrous promise. In Jesus' Name, I pray. Amen.

(2 Sam. 12: 25; Rev. 2: 17; Acts 13: 22; Luke 10: 20; Heb. 12: 23; Phil. 4: 3; Rev. 21: 17; Rev. 3: 5, 12; Is. 49: 16)

Father, as I quietly sit before You praying for my grandchildren, what meanings do their names hold? What is their essence, their character, and their reputation that is seen through Your divine lens? Is there any word, Scripture, or insight which concerns my grandchildren that You want to bring to my heart? I surrender my thoughts to You and I commit to pray in obedience to what You reveal.

Word:

Date:

Sharing Stories and Testimonies

Father, I love to read the Bible stories for I learn our family history. The Bible characters give me the example, encouragement, and strength to stand for You in any circumstance. I have my story to tell as well. My life has been written by Your hand ~ a life that was lost, sought out, and rescued. Your Word tells me to always be ready to give a defense to anyone who asks me to account for the hope that is in me. Father, would You present opportunity after opportunity which allow me to share my own compelling personal stories of faith with my grandchildren. I am in no way ashamed of what I believe, for the Gospel is Your power for salvation for anyone who believes. May my testimony of what You have done for me be that same power of salvation for my grandchildren. Father, give me eyes to see when the times are opportune. Keep me attentive to knowing when a door has been opened to teach Your ways to them. When I share family stories and anecdotes, may I include the lessons of faith which have been intertwined. The Proverbs instruct my grandchildren to come and listen to the wisdom of elders who will teach them to fear the LORD. May my grandchildren never forget the things they have been taught regarding my family's commitment to You. May they store Your faithfulness in their hearts from childhood, and they will be given the wisdom to receive the salvation that comes by trusting in Christ Jesus. Amen.

(1 Peter 3: 15; 2 Tim. 1: 12; Rom. 1: 16; Ps. 51: 13; Prov. 1: 8;
Ps. 34: 11; Prov. 3: 1; 2 Tim. 3: 15; Ps. 71: 17)

Father, as I sit quietly before You praying for my grandchildren, is there any word, Scripture, insight, or particular situation related to this topic which concerns my grandchildren that You want to bring to my heart? I surrender my thoughts to You and I commit to pray in obedience to what You reveal.

Word:

Date:

Teaching Constancy and Commitment

Heavenly Father, Your Word unveils Your divine essence of constancy. You are unchangeable, unwavering, immutable. You are stable, invariable, faithful, and deliberate. You are perpetually the same. Your wisdom is unchanging. You know as much now as ever ~ neither more nor less. Your Word is always true; it is impossible for You to lie. You are just and holy as You were in past generations. You vary not in Your goodness. Generosity and benevolence is Your nature.

Your Word also reveals permanent signs of Your covenant with mankind. You stand by Your covenants, remembering them forever. You have made a commitment to a thousand generations. You do not change Your plans. There is nothing that You begin to build and leave undone. You create worlds in Your hands. When You say it will be done, You never alter. Your purposes stand. You are unchangeable in Your promises. The Gospel is not promising today and denying tomorrow.

Father, my grandchildren live in a time when constancy and commitment are often absent. People bore easily, they discard the old, and they extol all things new. Many children are tossed about by rootlessness, rapid changes, and job transience. I need Your guidance in teaching my grandchildren that constancy and commitment are qualities to be valued. They will need to know how to remain true, constant, and faithful in a world where opportunities for vital commitments are fleeting. May I teach them how to be committed by my example. Allow me to demonstrate constancy in my dependence on You. I pray that in all circumstances I will set my face like flint and I will never be ashamed. I pray that I will demonstrate constancy in friendships. Help me teach my grandchildren how to pledge my friendship by being steady, nurturing, trustworthy, and accountable. Finally, I pray my grandchildren will learn how to maintain lifelong, loving marriages. May the married adults who surround them demonstrate what this sacred commitment entails. They will need to learn to be "other centered." They will need to make covenantal and unconditional promises. Their relationships will need to be built on steadfast love. May they learn forgiveness. May they bless others by giving their lives in mutual loving-kindness, tenderness, and submission. In all relationships may they demonstrate Your character of constancy and commitment. In Jesus' Name. Amen.

(Ex. 31: 17; 1 Chron. 16: 15; Ps. 105: 8; Is. 9:7; Tit. 1: 2; Is. 50: 7)

Father, as I sit quietly before You praying for my grandchildren, is there any word, Scripture, insight, or particular situation related to constancy and commitment which concerns my grandchildren that You want to bring to my heart? I surrender my thoughts to You and I commit to pray in obedience to what You reveal.

Word:

Date:

Teaching Courtesy and Respect

Father, I have observed my adult children teaching my grandchildren proper manners and etiquette. They are patient and persistent in guiding these little ones in being grateful for what they are given and in thinking of others besides themselves. My prayer is that my grandchildren will not only learn social comportment and polite behaviors, but that You will establish respect and courtesy in their hearts so that their outward behavior is truly a demonstration of an inward quality. May they develop an inner foundation of reverence. Reverence is one of the greatest virtues of childhood.

Help me teach my grandchildren Your command to consider the needs of others before their own. May they be humble, thinking of others as better than themselves. Your Word instructs them to respect and honor their parents and all will go well for them. You are pleased when children obey their parents. You teach them to honor those who are their leaders. Thank you that You structure authority so that children are relieved of the responsibility for mature judgment and decision before they are ready. Give them a willing obedience and submissive nature to appreciate and esteem authority.

Father, may my grandchildren never resort to flattery in order to gain something for themselves. May they refrain from using good manners to conceal greedy motives. You disdain empty flattery and pretense. May their hearts and motives be open and sincere. I pray that I will teach courtesy and respect to my grandchildren by demonstrating a genuine respect toward them in return. In Jesus' Name, I pray. Amen.

(Col. 3: 20; Heb. 12: 9; Phil. 2: 3; 1 Thess. 2: 5; Deut. 5: 16;
Matt. 15: 4; Matt. 19:19)

Father, as I sit quietly before You praying for my grandchildren, is there any word, Scripture, insight, or particular situation related to courtesy and respect which concerns my grandchildren that You want to bring to my heart? I surrender my thoughts to You and I commit to pray in obedience to what You reveal.

Word:

Date:

Rejoicing in the Lord - A Psalm

There are few things more satisfying than gardening as the sun comes up. A skunk cautiously shares my space (some distance away)! An army of industrious sugar ants keep me company. Black bumblebees zoom across my path. There are barn swallows nesting above our front door. I often have a beautiful fox that sits on our lawn while I work. This morning I am filled with gratitude and thankfulness - for belonging to a Savior such as ours, for being a part of a Body of Christ such as ours, for meaningful life work, for family and friends, health, a season for producing good fruit, for my grandchildren, promises for their future . . .

This is the day the Lord has made. I rejoice and I am glad in it! I rejoice in You always. And again I say, I rejoice! I delight myself in You, Lord. Happy am I because God is my LORD!

Father, thank You for loving my grandchildren and rejoicing over them with joy. They are redeemed. They will come with singing, and everlasting joy will be upon their heads. They will obtain joy and gladness, and sorrow and sighing will flee away. That spirit of rejoicing, joy, and laughter is their heritage. Where the Spirit of the Lord is, there is liberty - emancipation from bondage, freedom. They will walk in that liberty.

Father, I praise you with joyful lips. I am ever stimulated with the Holy Spirit. I speak out with psalms and hymns and make melody with all my heart to You. My grandchildren's happy hearts are good medicine and their cheerful minds work healing. The light in their eyes rejoice the heart of others. They have a good report. Their countenances radiate the joy of the Lord.

Father, I thank You that my grandchildren will bear much fruit. I ask in Jesus' Name, and I will receive, so that my joy may be full and overflowing. The joy of the Lord is my grandchildren's strength. Therefore, they will count it all joy, all strength, when they encounter tests or trials of any sort because they will be strong in You, Father.

They have the victory in the Name of Jesus. Satan is under their feet. They will not be moved by adverse circumstances. They will be made the righteousness of God in Christ Jesus. They dwell in the Kingdom of God and have peace and joy in the Holy Spirit. Praise the Lord! Again, I say, rejoice! Amen.

(Ps. 118: 24; Phil. 4: 4; Is. 62: 5; Is. 51: 11; 2 Cor. 3: 17; James 1: 2; Rom. 16: 20)

Father, as I sit quietly before You praying for my grandchildren, here are my own words of praise that I offer to You:

Date:

Leading a Grandchild to Christ

Heavenly Father, there will be a time when my grandchildren must make a decision for themselves to accept Jesus Christ. They have been brought up in a family with a rich Christian heritage, but they must make their own decision of whether or not You are the Savior of the world and Savior and Lord of their own lives. You have no grandchildren. Every person must make a personal choice to follow You and become Your child. The Bible says that a Christian is someone who walks in the way of life in contrast to the way of death. Jesus said, "I am the way and the truth and the life. No one comes to the Father except through Me." Jesus will not show them the way. He says, "I am the way."

Father, I pray for the persons who will lay the foundation and lead my grandchildren to make a choice to accept Jesus into their own hearts. That privilege may even be given to me, their grandparent. Jesus said, "The harvest is plentiful, but the workers are few. So pray to the Lord Who is in charge of the harvest; ask Him to send out more workers for His fields." My grandchildren will be wheat ripened and ready for Your harvest. I make myself available to You as a reaper. Your Word says that I should pray for many opportunities to preach the mystery of the Gospel ~ that Christ is for them. I pray that I will proclaim this message as clearly as I should. I ask You to give me the right words as I boldly explain Your secret plan of the Good News, preaching this message as Your ambassador.

When I pray, You answer me; You encourage me by giving me the strength I need. I pray that I will not be fearful of failure for I have received power from the Holy Spirit and I will be Your witness.

I pray I will not be fearful of rejection, for I know that the world hated You first. It is the work of the Holy Spirit to convict. Keep me from fearing that I do not have enough knowledge, for one thing I do know: I was blind and now I see.

By the empowerment of Your Holy Spirit, I will reveal to my grandchildren Your plan for them to fully experience the peace and life that only You can give. The Bible says, "For God so loved the world that He gave His only Son, so that everyone who believes in Him will not perish but have eternal life." They will need to know that "all have sinned; all fall short of God's glorious standard." "For the wages of sin is death, but the free gift of God is eternal life through Christ Jesus our Lord." May I present to them Your remedy ~ the Cross. When Jesus died on the cross and rose from the grave, He paid the penalty for their sins. And may I tell them of Your invitation to accept Christ's death on the cross as payment for their personal sins and to receive Jesus Christ as Savior and Lord. The Bible says, "But to all who believed Him and accepted Him, He gave the right to become children of God." My grandchildren will be found and "there will be great rejoicing in the presence of Your angels over one sinner who repents." I thank You in Jesus' Name. Amen.

(John 14: 6; Matt. 9: 37–38; Col. 4: 3–4; Eph 6: 19–20; Ps. 138: 3; Acts 1: 8; John 15: 18; 1 Thess. 1: 5; John 9: 25b; John 3: 16 NLT; Romans 3: 23 NLT; Rom. 6: 23 NLT; John 14: 6; Luke 15: 10 NLT)

A Prayer for Salvation

(a prayer for the grandchild to pray)

Heavenly Father, I want to be a real Christian. I realize that my sins have separated me from You. Please forgive me. I believe what Jesus did for me on the cross. He died to pay for the penalty of my sins. I don't completely understand it, but I accept it by faith. I do want to be a child of Yours, a member of Your family. Please come into my life, Lord Jesus, and make me Your child right now. I now turn from going my own way. I'll follow You and obey You for ever. Thank You for Your gift of eternal life and for Your Holy Spirit, Who has now come to live in me. Amen.

Common Terms that may be confusing to a youngster...

• Believe ~ trust, accept as true

• Born again, converted ~ changed, transformed, like a caterpillar to a butterfly

• Confess ~ admit

• Found the Lord, Get saved ~ accept what Christ offers, make a decision to follow Christ

• Grace ~ God's totally unearned forgiveness

• Repent ~ to be sorry about wrongs and turn from them

• Saved, salvation ~ forgiven of wrongs and given eternal life

• Sin ~ acting against God's will and offending God's character

• Testimony ~ story

• Witness ~ tell, show

Prayers for Events
and Holidays

- Life Events -

Birth of a Child

Heavenly Father,

This is the day You have made and I rejoice and am glad in it. This is the day You have precisely appointed for the birth of my grandchild! You chose this time and this season to establish Your purposes for this child's life and Your kingdom's expansion. I know that my grandchild is entering the world for such a time as this! May my daughter (daughter-in-law) not fear childbirth because she is fixed on You and trusts in Your goodness. Her pain will only be momentary compared to the joy which follows. I stand on Your kindness that the delivery of this grandbaby will be without complications. I ask for all decisions regarding the delivery and any related medical procedures to be covered by the inspiration of Your Holy Spirit who gives skill to the medical staff. Intervene, if necessary. Lord, You are my daughter's (daughter's-in-law) dwelling place. Your Word says that evil will not come near her and no infirmity will strike her or her unborn baby. This expectant mother knows that Jesus died on the cross to take away her sickness and pain. She has faith that her child will be born healthy and completely whole. Thank You for protecting her and my grandbaby's health through a safe delivery. I welcome this grandchild into the world and into my heart! In Jesus' Name. Amen.

(Ps. 118: 24; Esther 4: 14; Ps. 91: 5–7; Rom. 8: 2)

Father, I want to remember this day always. This is the day my grandchild entered this world to serve You.

Name:
Date of Birth:

Name:
Date of Birth:

Name:
Date of Birth:

Name:
Date of Birth:

Name:
Date of Birth:

Name:
Date of Birth:

Adoption

Heavenly Father, "adoption" is a precious concept to You. In love, Your unchanging plan was always to adopt us into Your own family by bringing us to Yourself through Jesus Christ. This gave You great pleasure. Through Your Word, I have learned the high privilege of adoption. I am Your honored child. In this same way, we embrace this long-awaited child into our family. We dedicate ourselves to see that this child has all the love, privileges, and position as a beloved son (daughter) as though my children were his natural parents. Our family was not complete until this child came into our lives.

Originally, we had an expectation in mind concerning children. Like Abram, we asked, "O Sovereign LORD, what good are all Your blessings when I don't even have a son?" You, Lord God, provided more than we could have dreamed. As Your Word reveals, "All of these past saints received Your approval because of their faith, yet none of them received all that You had promised. For You had far better things in mind for them." My daughter (daughter-in-law) waited for You to answer her prayer. And You, Who are always faithful, give grace and glory. No good thing will You withhold from those who do what is right. You gave us a child to love. Bless this child, Lord God. Break forever any notion this child might carry of not having been wanted. Bless his birth parents and be merciful to them. Let them know that their child is cherished by another family who will do all they can to raise him in a circle of love which originates in the heart of the Father. I pray this with gratitude in the Name of Your Son. Amen.

(Eph. 1: 5; Gen 15: 2 NLT; Heb. 11: 39–40; Ps. 84: 11)

Grandchild's name:

Date of Birth:

Father, as I sit quietly before You praying for my grandchildren, is there any word, Scripture, insight, or particular situation related to this topic which concerns my newly adopted grandchild that You want to bring to my heart? I surrender my thoughts to You and I commit to pray in obedience to what You reveal. May You break any stronghold or negative thinking in my grandchild which will convey abandonment and/or illegitimacy.

Word:

Date:

Birthdays

O God, our times are in Your hands. In Your book all the days of our lives were written before they ever took shape, when as yet there was not one of them. Look with favor, I pray, on Your servant, my grandchild, as he begins another year. Grant that he may grow in wisdom and grace, and strengthen his trust in Your goodness. Watch over Your child, O Lord, as his days increase; bless and guide him wherever he may be. May he be happy in his faith and glad-hearted always. I pray that my grandchildren will be unceasing in prayer, thanking You in everything, no matter what the circumstances may be, for this is Your will for those who belong to Christ Jesus. Strengthen him when he stands; comfort him when discouraged or sorrowful; raise him up if he falls; and in his heart may Your peace which passes all understanding abide all the days of his life; through Jesus Christ our Lord. Amen.

(Adapted from the Book of Common Prayer)

Name:
Birthdate:

Name:
Birthdate:

Name:
Birthdate:

Name:
Birthdate:

Name:
Birthdate:

Name:
Birthdate:

Name:
Birthdate:

Name:
Birthdate:

Baptism

Note: We grandparents represent many denominations, and we practice the Holy Sacrament of Baptism in different ways. We all agree that Holy Baptism is full initiation by water and the Holy Spirit into Christ's Body, the universal Church. Some of our babies and young children will be baptized while they are yet unable to understand the significance of the vows made on their behalf. They will be represented by sponsors, parents, and Godparents, who commit to bring them up in the Christian faith, teaching them God's Word, prayers, the sacraments, and the importance of fellowship with other believers until that time when they make a public commitment of faith on their own. For our grandchildren who are older and understand the vows they are making, we join as witnesses of their proclamation of faith doing all in our power to support these children in their life in Christ. Let us pray that all our grandchildren will be baptized into the Christian faith, that each will make a public statement of faith, naming Jesus Christ as Savior and as Lord.

"I baptize you with water. But One more powerful than I will come, the thongs of whose sandals I am not worthy to untie. He will baptize you with the Holy Spirit and with fire." Luke 3: 16 NIV

And then He told them, "Go into all the world and preach the Good News to everyone, everywhere. Anyone who believes and is baptized will be saved. Mark 16: 15–16a NIV

Peter replied, "Each of you must turn from your sins and turn to God, and be baptized in the name of Jesus Christ for the forgiveness of your sins. Then you will receive the gift of the Holy Spirit. Acts 2: 38 NLT

But now the people believed Philip's message of Good News concerning the Kingdom of God and the name of Jesus Christ. As a result, many men and women were baptized. Acts 8: 12 NLT

One of them was Lydia from Thyatira, a merchant of expensive purple cloth. She was a worshiper of God. As she listened to us, the Lord opened her heart, and she accepted what Paul was saying. She was baptized along with other members of her household, Acts 16: 14–15 NLT

Crispus, the leader of the synagogue, and all his household believed in the Lord. Many others in Corinth also became believers and were baptized. Acts 18: 8 NLT

Paul said, "John's baptism was to demonstrate a desire to turn from sin and turn to God. John himself told the people to believe in Jesus, the One John said would come later." As soon as they heard this, they were baptized in the name of the Lord Jesus. Acts 19: 5 NLT

And now, why delay? Get up and be baptized, and have your sins washed away, calling on the name of the Lord. Acts 22: 16 NLT
Some of us are Jews, some are Gentiles, some are slaves, and some are free. But we have all been baptized into Christ's body by one Spirit, and we have all received the same Spirit. 1 Cor. 12: 13 NLT

And all who have been united with Christ in baptism have been made like Him. Gal 3: 27 NLT

Heavenly Father, I present my grandchildren to You as they receive the Sacrament of Holy Baptism. I will join with their parents in seeing that they are brought up in the Christian faith and life. With Your help, I and my grandchildren renounce Satan and all the spiritual forces of wickedness that rebel against You. I and my grandchildren renounce the evil powers of this world which corrupt and destroy Your creations. I and my grandchildren renounce all sinful desires that draw us from our love of You. We turn to Jesus Christ and accept Him as our Savior. We put our whole trust in His grace and love. We promise to follow and obey Him as Lord. We will persevere in resisting evil, and whenever we fall into sin, we will repent and return to You. We will proclaim by word and example the Good News. We will seek and serve Christ in all persons, loving our neighbors as ourselves. We will not forget we are baptized to become one with Christ Jesus and that the public ceremony represents our death in Him and our rising to new life.

We thank You for the gift of water. Over it the Holy Spirit moved in the beginning of creation. Through it You led the children of Israel out of bondage into the land of promise. In it Your Son Jesus received the baptism of John and was anointed by the Holy Spirit as the Messiah to lead us through His death and resurrection, from the bondage of sin into everlasting life. May my grandchildren be reborn of the Spirit. May they be cleansed from their sin and born again into the risen life of Jesus Christ. Sustain them, O Lord, in Your Holy Spirit. Give them inquiring and discerning hearts, the courage to will and to persevere, a spirit to know and love You, and the gift of joy and wonder in all Your works. Seal them by the Holy Spirit in Baptism and mark them as Your own forever. May they share in the royal priesthood of Jesus Christ. Amen.

(adapted from The Book of Common Prayer)

Name:
Date of Baptism:

Name:
Date of Baptism:

Name:
Date of Baptism:

Name:
Date of Baptism:

Name:
Date of Baptism:

Name:
Date of Baptism:

Name:
Date of Baptism:

Dedication

Lord, just as Hannah prayed for Samuel, Mary prayed for Jesus, and Eunice and Lois prayed for Timothy, I prayed for my grandchildren before they were even born. In Your great mercy, You have granted my requests. You have brought a new child into my family, a child that I love and will grow to cherish. Now I lift this grandchild in prayer before Your altar to give him back to You. Everything comes from You–and I am giving You only what Your love has given to my family. In deep gratitude, my heart recognizes that my grandchild is a gift from Your hand. You have given my family a blessing, a reward, and a heritage. You promised that children would be a fruitful vine within our home; children would be like olive shoots around the table of my family. My heart bows in humility at this honor.

I not only dedicate this newest grandchild, but each of the others and my entire family to You and to Your service. We will need divine wisdom in raising these precious gifts of Your grace. We commit to raise them in the fear and admonition of the Lord. We will teach them from the day they are born to seek You with all their heart, soul, mind, and strength. As a grandparent committed to Jesus Christ, I promise to do my best to inscribe Your commandments on their hearts. I consecrate myself and my grandchildren to You–and I will wait and watch in faith for You to do amazing things in transforming their lives. Keep me and their parents from holding on, and give us grace to release them back to You though we may want to cling.

Thank You, LORD, for choosing my own children as caretakers and me as a doting grandparent of these precious lives. As I ponder the miracle of their presence in my life, I dedicate my grandchildren to You, confident not in myself, but in Your wonderful faithfulness to mould them into devoted followers who will bring glory to Your Name. In Jesus' Name, I pray. Amen.

(1 Sam. 1:28; 1 Chron. 29: 14; Ps. 127:3; Deut. 4:29; James 1:5; Deut. 6: 7–8; Josh. 3:5; Ps. 116:12–14; 2 Tim. 2: 13)

Father, as I sit quietly before You praying for my grandchildren, is there any word, Scripture, insight, or particular situation related to this topic which concerns my newly dedicated grandchild that You want to bring to my heart? I surrender my thoughts to You and I commit to pray in obedience to what You reveal.

Word:

Date:

Salvation Day

Almighty God, Lord of all Creation, Savior, Redeemer, and King:

This day, all of heaven rejoices for my grandchild has been found. The Bible describes through parables what it is like in heaven when one of Your children cries out, "I receive Jesus Christ as my Savior and Lord!" In the story of the lost sheep, Jesus said, "Suppose one of you has a hundred sheep and loses one of them. Does he not leave the ninety-nine in the open country and go after the lost sheep until he finds it? And when he finds it, he joyfully puts it on his shoulders, calls his friends and neighbors together and says, 'Rejoice with me; I have found my lost sheep.' I tell you that in the same way there will be more rejoicing in heaven over one sinner who repents than over ninety-nine righteous persons who do not need to repent." The woman who found her lost coin called her friends and neighbors together and said, "Rejoice with me; I have found my lost coin." In the same way, You tell us, there is rejoicing in the presence of Your angels over one sinner who repents.

The father in the parable of the prodigal son reveals to us Your heart: "The father said to his servants, 'Quick! Bring the best robe and put it on him. Put a ring on his finger and sandals on his feet. Bring the fattened calf and kill it. Let's have a feast and celebrate. For this son of mine was dead and is alive again; he was lost and is found.' So they began to celebrate."

Father, all heaven is celebrating. My grandchild has been received into the Kingdom. We drive a stake into the ground to remind us that this is the day my grandchild made a decision to follow Jesus Christ. He will dwell with Him forever. Help him to share his newfound faith with his family and friends. Help him to read

Your Word and saturate himself with truth so that his thoughts and emotions will be changed. Allow him to meet other Christians and be received into a church. Teach him to build communication with You through prayer. Continually give him evidence that new, good things are being added to his life and old things are passing away. Establish him by the power of Your Spirit.

Behold, You stood at the door and knocked. My grandchild heard Your Voice and opened the door. You came in to him. Thank You, God, for answering my prayer. In Jesus' Name, I pray. Amen.

(Luke 15 NLT; Rev. 3: 20)

Name:

Date accepted Jesus as Lord:

Name:

Date accepted Jesus as Lord:

Name:

Date accepted Jesus as Lord:

- School -

First Day of School

Father, it is time to release my grandchild into the care of another. His parents have instilled in him a love for You and a love for others. He will take this knowledge with him as he enters a classroom with unknown expectations. Guard his heart, Lord God. Watch over him to protect his curious mind from false and worldly philosophies which are meant to discredit Your Word. I pray his teacher will be a follower of Jesus Christ. If this is not possible, then my prayer is for other Believers to look after him each day at school. I pray his teachers will purpose to inspire him, challenge him, encourage him to grow, and protect him from the abuses of others. May his teachers see what I see in this child ~ unique qualities and abilities that need encouragement, training, and godly direction. May he be a respecter of authority. May he understand that You have placed responsible adults in charge over his life for his welfare and well-being. Give him courage to face an unknown environment, a curious and disciplined mind to study and analyze his lessons, and an obedient and teachable heart to learn what You open to his understanding. Father, on this important beginning to this child's life, I pray my grandchild will be filled with the knowledge of Your will; have all spiritual wisdom and understanding; live a life worthy of You; please You in every way; bear fruit in every good work; grow in his knowledge of You; and be strengthened with all power according to Your glorious might. In Jesus' Name, I pray. Amen.

(Colossians 1: 9–11)

Name of grandchild:
Name of School:
Teachers to pray for:
Date of School Year:

Name of grandchild:
Name of School:
Teachers to pray for:
Date of School Year:

Name of grandchild:
Name of School:
Teachers to pray for:
Date of School Year:

Name of grandchild:
Name of School:
Teachers to pray for:
Date of School Year:

School Days

Father, in Jesus' Name, I confess Your Word concerning my grandchildren as they attend school each day. I know that You walk with them into each classroom, and You open their minds to learning. You watch over them on the playground and You bring companions their way with whom they can run and play. Your Spirit hovers over them creating within them the power and desire to please You. If they pay attention to His inner stirring and carefully follow the commands of the LORD, Your Word promises that my grandchildren will always be at the top, never at the bottom. You will make them the head and not the tail, above and not beneath. I know that this does not mean they will always make the highest grades or be chosen for honors or be appointed captain of the team, but You will allow them to find favor with teachers and classmates, and they will find favor with You.

Please help my grandchildren recognize the value of their education and the merit of rigorous training ~ in school, in Sunday School, in extracurricular activities, in sports. May they be diligent in their study, and curious of the broad and wonderful world around them. I will not cease to pray for them, asking that they be filled with the knowledge of Your will, bearing fruit in every good work. I will pray for their protection from exposure to materials that do not reflect godly values. Thank You for the angels whom You assign to them to accompany, defend, and preserve them in all their ways of obedience as they follow You. You will oppose those who oppose these children. You will put on Your spear and javelin, take up Your shield, and come to the aid of my grandchildren when they are in harm's way.

I pray for godly men and women of integrity to be their teachers and mentors. Grant these adults a fear of the Lord and divine wisdom in order that they may walk in the ways of reverence and purity, honoring Your Name. May they consider their role of teacher as a high calling to serve the King. May my grandchildren's teachers, mentors, and coaches be adults who refrain from immorality and all sexual looseness ~ flee from impurity in thought, word, and deed ~ living and conducting themselves honorably as in the open light of day.

I ask You to seal the work of the Holy Spirit in the lives of my grandchildren this school year. Would You seal the wisdom and spiritual understanding they will receive in all areas of study and endeavor. I pray that You will not allow the enemy to steal or rob or pillage anything that is of You. May their teachers carry my grandchildren in their hearts. Bless them for pouring out their lives on my grandchildren's behalf. And at the close of the school year, would You say to the hearts of these educators that You have seen their good work and in them You are well pleased. I pray this in Jesus' Name. Amen.

(Deut. 28: 13; Ps. 111: 10; Prov. 1: 7; Prov. 9: 10; Ps. 35: 1–2; Ps. 91: 11; Eph. 3: 17; Prov. 4: 18)

Father, as I sit quietly before You praying for my grandchildren, is there any word, Scripture, insight, or particular situation related to this topic which concerns my grandchild that You want to bring to my heart? I surrender my thoughts to You and I commit to pray in obedience to what You reveal.

Word:

Date:

Academic Problems

Heavenly Father, my precious grandchild is struggling in school. My heart hurts for her. I ask You to break any cycle of discouragement, disappointment, and failure. Would You replace this pattern with a season of new possibilities. You are the One Who sets prisoners free. Release this child, Lord! The assumption that this child will fail blinds her to new possibilities that You have for her. She thinks she cannot learn, and this keeps her from knowing what she cannot yet see. Her teachers, her parents, and her classmates may only see her weaknesses. You see the strengths You gave her to bring honor to Your Name. Others see what this child has done so far in her class work. You see what she is capable of doing with patient training and a little more time. This grandchild sees why she cannot do things; You see how she can. She is beginning to believe her current limitations. You have vision of Your resources that will give her strength. Her parents, teachers, and classmates see only the problems; You provide the inspired solutions.

Father, give my grandchild eyes of faith to believe in possibility. Silence those voices that speak discouragement and failure. Awaken in her the courage to take risks in trying again. I know that You gently lead those whose hearts are wounded, and I pray You will guide her with Your counsel, ministering hope to her spirit. In Jesus' Name. Amen.

(Ps. 73: 24; Phil 4: 13; Heb. 11: 34; 1 Cor. 1: 27; 2 Cor. 12: 10)

Father, as I sit quietly before You praying for my grandchildren, is there any word, Scripture, insight, or particular situation related to this topic which concerns my grandchildren that You want to bring to my heart? I surrender my thoughts to You and I commit to pray in obedience to what You reveal.

Word:

Date:

Choosing a College

Thank You, Father, that You have placed an important decision before my grandchild concerning his college and preparation for his future. His friends are already receiving acceptances, and I know he is anxious to secure his place as well. In the flesh, he may rush to decide what to do before placing the choices before You. Hold my grandchild back from presumption, Lord. Give him a steady heart to reflect on Your will for his life. His choice will most likely determine what occupation he will have, what city he will live in, and which person he will marry. This is a very important decision and needs Your guidance. I ask You to help my grandchild consider all aspects, evaluating both the positive and negative of each college. If he does not immediately hear from You, Father, he may slip into laziness thinking he can stop praying, for perhaps You are withholding Your answer to his request. His faith need not be discouraged by delay. He will need to learn that prayer must often be gathered up until the time is right. May he wait in quiet confidence in persevering prayer. The blessing of Your answer is all prepared. You will not delay a moment longer than necessary, knowing the exact moment when his spirit is ripe in the fullness of faith to take and keep the blessing You have in store. Help him, Father, to hear Your Voice, and then to make the right and correct choice. Prevent him from not only acting in haste, but also from delaying too long to reach his conclusion. Help him not to be influenced by outside pressure of friends or family, the reputation he desires, the easiest and most familiar route, or his own preferences. May he use this decision to yield to Your purpose for his future. Keep him from the fear of being overlooked, and help him focus on what pleases You. Your promised answer not only will give him the desire of his heart, but also a blessed future he cannot even begin to imagine. In Jesus' Name. Amen.

(1 Chron 28: 20; Ps. 139: 23; Prov. 12: 25; Phil 4: 6; Eph. 3: 20; Rom. 15: 4–5; Rom. 5: 3–4; Heb. 10: 35–37; Heb. 6: 12; Rom. 8: 24–25)

Father, as I sit quietly before You praying for my grandchildren, is there any word, Scripture, insight, or particular situation related to this topic or any decision my grandchild must make that You want to bring to my heart? I surrender my thoughts to You and I commit to pray in obedience to what You reveal.

Word:

Date:

Graduation

Heavenly Father, I acknowledge that riches and honor come from You alone, for You rule over everything. Power and might are in Your hand, and it is at Your discretion that people are made great and given strength. O God, I thank You and praise Your glorious name! You tell us not to be proud and not to trust in our wealth which will soon be gone. Our trust should be in the living God, who richly gives us all we need for our enjoyment. On this day, Father, I want to honor my grandchild on his achievement in graduating from (high school, college, or professional school). He has worked hard to arrive at this distinction, and I ask Your blessing on his perseverance. I thank You for this honor, this diploma. Help my grandchild to remember that regardless of his education and skill, it is You, God, Who gives him the power to make wealth. Pride goes before destruction, and haughtiness before a fall. He will remain humble before You. He will not conquer the land with his sword; it was not his own strength that gave him victory. It was by your mighty power that he succeeded; it was because You favored him and smiled on him. May he enjoy this moment of celebrating his accomplishments. And at the close of the day, may my grandchild humbly kneel down before You, thanking You for providing his education, his experiences ~ good and bad, his friends and support systems, his opportunities, and his hope for his future. In Jesus' Name, I pray. Amen.

(1 Tim. 6: 17; 1 Chron. 29: 12–13;; Deut. 8: 18; Prov. 16: 18 NLV;
Ps. 44: 3; Prov. 22: 4: Jer. 9: 23–24; Gal. 6: 14; Eze. 36: 37;
1 Cor. 3: 7)

Father, as I sit quietly before You praying for my grandchildren, is there any word, Scripture, insight, or particular situation related to this topic on graduation that You want to bring to my heart? I surrender my thoughts to You and I commit to pray in obedience to what You reveal.

Word:

Date:

- Activities -

Musical, Artistic, and Special Abilities

Heavenly Father, I recognize that You have given my grand-children special creative abilities which they will use in the service of the King. These gifts of creativity will forward Your kingdom through music, drama, dance, graphic arts, writing skills, painting, sewing, and sculpting. Bezalel and Oholiab were *"filled with the Spirit of God, with skill, ability and knowledge in all kinds of crafts to make artistic designs for work in gold, silver, and bronze, to cut and set stones, to work in wood and to engage in all kinds of artistic craftsmanship. They were skilled to do all kinds of work as craftsmen, designers, embroiderers in blue, purple and scarlet yarn and fine linen, and weavers."*

David was uniquely gifted as a musician, *"the man anointed by the God of Jacob, Israel's beloved singer of songs."* David's great poetic ability was a skill You used to enhance temple worship then, and all through the ages that followed. *Heman and Jeduthun were responsible for the sounding of the trumpets and cymbals and for the playing of the other instruments for sacred song.* The Old Testament mentions those artists who were regularly called to their craft. *"Those who were musicians, heads of the Levite families, stayed in the rooms of the temple and were exempt from other duties because they were responsible for the work day and night."* Further, Scripture mentions the training of artists, recognizing the importance of this ministry.

Thank You for the gifts given to my grandchildren ~ many which have not yet been revealed. Help my grandchildren to develop these abilities and gifts, to create without hesitation. May they visualize, compose, and develop thoughts and language when their minds are allowed to wander and dream. May they solve their creative problems when they awaken at night, recognizing the answers or inspiration as a prompting of the Holy Spirit. May they take thoughts and sound and shape and form, which You have created, and combine them into expressions which glorify You and enhance worship throughout the world.

I pray my grandchildren will use their particular creative ability to benefit the Body of Christ. May they never confuse their spiritual gifts for a natural talent and use them for self-glory. I pray they will not fail to develop their gift through laziness or inattention or lack of discipline. May they never harbor pride in their ability nor show false humility. Keep them from a fear of failure which might prohibit them from expressing their inspiration. May they refrain from jealousy of another's talent. Help our family and their teachers to recognize and encourage the artistic and musical abilities demonstrated in my grandchildren. I thank You for their Spirit-given talents and gifts, and I pray that they will be used for Your glory. In Jesus' Name. Amen.

(Exodus 35: 31–35 NIV; 2 Samuel 23:1 NIV;
1 Chronicles 16: 41–42 NLT; 2 Chronicles 5: 12–13;
1 Chronicles 9: 33 NIV; 1 Chronicles 25: 6–7)

Father, as I sit quietly before You praying for my grandchildren, is there any word, Scripture, insight, or particular situation related to talents and abilities which concerns my grandchildren that You want to bring to my heart? I surrender my thoughts to You and I commit to pray in obedience to what You reveal.

Word:

Date:

Extra-curricular Activities

Father, be with my grandchildren as they participate in sports, in drama, in riding lessons, in dance or ballet, art classes, scouts, or any activity outside of their regular classes. I know that these are graces that You extend to these children to broaden their experience and experiment with their talents and unique abilities. I ask for balance in the time they spend studying, exercising, and attending other programs after school. Keep them from being overwhelmed with too busy a schedule. You will want time with them each day. For that to happen, their parents will need to model a life that puts You first. They will need to learn that nothing is more important than sitting at the feet of the Master, listening to what He teaches. As my grandchildren return home after a full day of learning, dust off the world, Lord God, and call them into that private communion with You where they can be refreshed. Minister to any woundedness that they received from the day. Speak Your love into their hearts. And before they lay down to sleep, may their final thoughts be of You and Your unconditional love, goodness, and grace. Unless You, LORD, build the house, they labor in vain who build it; unless You, LORD, guard the city, the watchman stays awake in vain. It is vain to rise up early, to sit up late, to eat the bread of sorrows. You give Your beloved sleep. At the end of the day, may my grandchildren lie down in peace, and sleep; for You alone, O LORD, make them dwell in safety. Amen.

(Luke 10: 39; Ps. 4: 8, Ps. 127: 1–3 NASB)

Father, as I sit quietly before You praying for my grandchildren, is there any word, Scripture, insight, or particular situation related to this topic which concerns my grandchildren that You want to bring to my heart? I surrender my thoughts to You and I commit to pray in obedience to what You reveal.

Word:

Date:

Team Sports

Father, my grandchild has reached the age that she can participate in various team sports. Thank You for her coordination and athleticism. She will learn lessons as an athlete which she will take with her through her life. Of course, a grandparent's first concern is for the safety of the grandchild. Would You give Your angels charge over my grandchild's life to protect her from injury. Keep her from carelessness and inattention; may her coaches and trainers supervise and provide the needed exercise program geared to keeping children in good physical shape. Knowing that You watch over her physical well-being, I pray concerning her character. Thank You, Father, that my grandchild will learn discipline and dedication. She will experience teamwork and unity that develops among those seeking a common goal. She will learn to take instruction and direction from those in authority. She will also learn to withstand criticism and correction without resentment. Keep her teachable, Lord. She will learn to receive honors with genuine humility, recognizing that others helped her to win the prize. She will not garner glory for herself, but will see the value of leadership and team effort. And when she loses, she will learn to respond with integrity and self-control. Your Word gives many examples of persevering in the faith as an athlete perseveres in the field. May my grandchild apply all she learns from sports to her faith walk with You. Help her to remember that in a race everyone runs, but only one person gets the prize. She also must run in such a way that she will win. All athletes practice strict self-control. They do it to win a prize that will fade away, but my grandchild will persevere for an eternal prize. May she always remember, since she is surrounded by such a great cloud of witnesses, to throw off everything that hinders and the sin that so easily entangles, and to run with perseverance the race marked out for her. May she know the true race she is running, forgetting what is behind and straining toward what is ahead. Grant that my grandchild will press on toward the goal to win the prize for which You have called her heavenward in Christ Jesus. Amen.

(Ps. 91: 11–12; 1 Cor. 9: 24–25; Heb. 12:1; Phil. 3: 13–14)

Father, as I sit quietly before You praying for my grandchildren, is there any word, Scripture, insight, or particular situation related to this topic on team sports which concerns my grandchildren that You want to bring to my heart? I surrender my thoughts to You and I commit to pray in obedience to what You reveal.

Word:

Date:

Sunday School and Church Activities

Father, in the Name of Jesus, I bless the work of the Sunday School staff which dedicates itself to teaching my grandchildren. Thank you for the many volunteers who have a passion for children and a vision to see my grandchildren grow into fully devoted followers of Jesus Christ. I pray that these volunteers will model a zeal for Jesus that is contagious. Provide Your authority and leadership in this ministry. Please continue to direct the staff to age appropriate materials and projects that will build my grandchildren's enthusiasm for spiritual things. Lord, give this ministry team clear direction from You, and make their hearts teachable in order to pass that quality on to the children entrusted to their care. May these teachers be filled with the Holy Spirit. May they employ their gifts of the Spirit providing wisdom and encouragement, knowledge and leadership, administration and hospitality, craftsmanship and musical ability, in order to devise creative methods for teaching my grandchildren Your Word and Your character. Thank You that these teachers are perfecting and fully equipping these little saints. Thank You that my grandchildren are learning to worship and to pray.

Father, You will teach Youth Ministry leaders to listen to the cries of these young people they serve. Give them an ear that hears a clarion call for this generation. Father, forgive us for mistakes we adults have made out of our own unresolved hurts or selfishness which have caused today's youth to be wounded. I release the anointing that is upon Jesus to bind up and heal my grandchildren's broken hearts and the hearts of their friends. Thank You for the Holy Spirit Who will lead them into all truth and correct erroneous perceptions about past or present situations. Thank You for that special gifting youth ministers have to relate to young people.

Finally, I ask You to help the children and youth who attend Sunday School and other youth activities to submit to their youth leaders, youth pastors, teachers, and mentors. The first commandment with a promise is to the child who obeys her parents in the Lord. You said that all will be well with these children and they will live long on the earth. I affirm this promise on behalf of my grandchildren. I ask You to give them obedient spirits that they may honor and esteem their teachers and leaders. Thank You each time my grandchildren meet with other young people to learn about You. In Jesus' Name, I pray. Amen.

Father, as I sit quietly before You praying for my grandchildren, is there any word, Scripture, insight, or particular situation related to Sunday School or church which concerns my grandchildren that You want to bring to my heart? I surrender my thoughts to You and I commit to pray in obedience to what You reveal.

Word:

Date:

- Away From Home -

Summer Camp

Father, thank You for the summer opportunities that You make available to my grandchildren. You use these times to grow them physically, emotionally, and spiritually. I thank You for the camp (or program) my adult children have thoughtfully and prayerfully chosen for my grandchildren to attend. Thank You that the summer staff has already been hired, including enthusiastic college age students who love Jesus. May they all have a love for children and zeal to see them grow towards maturity in Christ.

The camp leadership team will have many needs, for which I pray. The buildings and grounds team will be completing many projects before the children arrive in order for the campers to be safe. Give them wisdom and unity of spirit to identify and resolve any problems that could be potential hazards. I pray for the food service department which will prepare nutritional meals and give my grandchildren something to complain about! Isn't that what children do at camp, Lord? I pray for the staff preparing outdoor and indoor activities. May their offerings be stimulating and challenging for my grandchildren. I pray for the counselors of every cabin or building to be emotionally and spiritually healthy. May they enjoy my grandchildren and identify ways to push them out of their comfort zone. I pray for the friends and cabin mates my grandchildren will encounter. You will arrange for them to meet all kinds of people, some which will become their best friends and some whom they'll want to ignore. Teach my grandchildren Your heart for people, and encourage them by Your Spirit to notice those who are left out. May my grandchildren lay down their wants and preferences to be a companion to someone who needs a friend. I pray my grandchildren will take no part in forming cliques, but will always extend themselves as You extend Yourself to all people. My grandchildren will be homesick at times, but You will remind them of Your Presence that is always with them.

Keep them safe, Lord. And bring them back to their family sun-burned, mosquito-bitten, scuff-knee'ed, sugar-deprived, and filled with stories of their summer adventures. In Jesus' Name, I pray. Amen.

(Acts 3: 20; Deut. 31: 6)

Father, as I sit quietly before You praying for my grandchildren, is there any word, Scripture, insight, or particular situation related to this topic on summer camp which concerns my grandchildren that You want to bring to my heart? I surrender my thoughts to You and I commit to pray in obedience to what You reveal.

Word:

Name of Camp:
Date:

Family Vacation

They're off, Lord! They have packed their bags, stowed their gear, checked their maps, and are on their way. My heart is glad, for I know this trip will bring them much needed rest from their busy schedule. You instituted many laws that had to do with rest. You knew we would work too hard and neglect to spend time replenishing our souls. You rested on the seventh day. You instituted the Sabbath rest. You had days of rest at the beginning and end of the harvest festivals. You even required that the land have a year of rest. When the Israelites set out from the mountain of the LORD and traveled for three days, the ark of the covenant went before them during those three days to find them a place to rest. I pray that Your Presence will go with my family, and You will give them rest.

Lord, I pray that this vacation will provide time for their parents to enjoy my grandchildren. Would You bring opportunities to them to truly listen and engage. Open their ears to hear what is on the hearts of my grandchildren. Help them discern the things that concern them, excite them, challenge them, and nourish them. You are able to orchestrate moments for these parents to be alone with each child in order to bless her individually. Give them teaching moments. New experiences provide openings to discover and consider ideas and places and people they have never encountered. I also pray that my adult children will use this vacation to teach my grandchildren new truths about Your character. Remind them to pray, even while they are vacationing. Remind them to study Your Word and to listen to Your Voice. While they travel, may they dwell in the shelter of the Most High and rest in the shadow of the Almighty. You will bring health and healing; You will heal Your people and will let them enjoy abundant peace and security. My children and grandchildren will trust in You and do well; they will dwell in the land and enjoy safe pasture. However many years they may live, let them enjoy them all. In Jesus' Name. Amen.

(Ex. 33: 14; Lev. 23: 29; Lev. 25: 5; Num. 10: 33; Ps. 91: 1; Matt. 11: 29; Ps. 37: 3; Eccl. 5: 19; Jer. 33: 6; Eccl. 11: 8)

Father, as I sit quietly before You praying for my grandchildren, is there any word, Scripture, insight, or particular situation related to this topic on vacations which concerns my grandchildren that You want to bring to my heart? I surrender my thoughts to You and I commit to pray in obedience to what You reveal.

Word:

Date:

Vacation Bible School

"Enlarge the place of your tent, stretch your tent curtains wide; do not hold back; lengthen your cords, strengthen your stakes. For you will spread out to the right and to the left . . ."Isaiah 54: 2–3

"Out of the mouths of babes and unweaned infants You have established strength because of Your foes, that You might silence the enemy and the avenger." Psalm 8:2

Father, my grandchildren are looking forward to Vacation Bible School. Thank You for the hours of preparation that have been expended in getting ready for this fun-filled week. Would You enable the leaders to be kind and welcoming as they greet my grandchildren. Let the leaders rejoice in their childlike qualities. May everyone involved make connections with one another (kids and adults) in Your Name. Let the adults be constantly gentle and dependent on You, Lord. When they run up against obstacles and problems each morning (which are sure to arise) let them turn to You immediately. And please let them share their prayers with the children who are always watching to find their way.

May the children attending come to know You in a whole new way, as their Father Who knows them better than anyone else, and Who is always there, waiting to step in and comfort them at any time they ask. May they all become more familiar with living an empowered and surrendered life of patience, love, and compassion. May Your Church and Kingdom be extended this week as a result of this event. May families feel welcomed and loved at their church. In Jesus' Name, I pray. Amen.

Father, as I sit quietly before You praying for my grandchildren, is there any word, Scripture, insight, or particular situation related to this topic on Vacation Bible School which concerns my grandchildren that You want to bring to my heart? I surrender my thoughts to You and I commit to pray in obedience to what You reveal.

Word:

Date:

Running Away

Father, I received word today that my grandchild wants to run away from home. How often I have wanted to do the same! If only I could pack a knapsack with a sandwich, a jar of lemonade, my $.15 savings, and my favorite stick and leave the pressing needs I face behind. Your prophet Elijah ran away. He went alone into the desert, sat under a solitary broom tree, and prayed that he might die. "I have had enough, Lord." He ran away for forty days and forty nights. Jonah ran away. When You gave him a command to follow, he got up and went in the opposite direction in order to get away from You. Jonah went down to the seacoast, to the port of Joppa, where he found a ship leaving for Tarshish. He bought a ticket and went on board, hoping that by going away to the west he could escape. Cleopas and his companion ran away. After Your Son's crucifixion, they left for Emmaus instead of Jerusalem disregarding what they had been instructed. Their hopes had been dashed and they wanted to go away ~ anywhere but Jerusalem ~ until You appeared on the road on which they traveled.

Why is my grandchild running away, Father? Is he frightened like Elijah, stubborn like Jonah, disappointed like Cleopas? You know why he feels disconnected to his family and wants to run away. Father, I know You will meet him on his journey down the street. I know You will remind him of his value and position within his home. If he feels neglected and ignored, would You inspire his parents to think of ways to reestablish communication. If he feels there has been an injustice and he has been wrongfully accused, he will need to know that Your Son was also accused yet died for His accusers. Would You shine truth that has not yet been revealed on any situation which troubles this child. If he feels ashamed and does not want to face the consequences of his actions, give him the grace to accept his parents' wisdom and discipline. Father, as You did with Elijah, I know You will go to any means to provide spiritual nourishment and strengthening for my grandchild. As you did with Jonah, You will pursue him even into the sea. As you did with Cleopas and his friend, You will meet my grandchild on his journey south in order to reveal Your Son to him. You will not be slow to act, Lord God. Give my grandchild's parents the discernment to know how to love this child back to fellowship with them and with You. And keep *me* from running away, Lord. Make me an obedient servant ready to respond to Your beckoning. In Jesus' Name, I pray. Amen.

(1 Kings 19; Jonah 1: 3; Luke 24: 13–33)

Father, as I sit quietly before You praying for my grandchildren, is there any word, Scripture, insight, or particular situation related to this topic which concerns my grandchildren that You want to bring to my heart? I surrender my thoughts to You and I commit to pray in obedience to what You reveal.

Word:

Date:

- Family Crisis -

Death of a Loved One

Father, my grandchildren are grieving. They have experienced the loss of someone very dear. You are always ready to extend Your consolation. Jesus wept at the loss of his friend. Your Word says, "Precious in the sight of the LORD is the death of His saints." I know that You understand their grief. I pray that these children would receive Your mercy and find grace in this time of need. Do not hide Yourself from their supplications. Fear and trembling have come upon them, horror and fright overcome them. I call on You to rescue them. You redeem life from the battle of hopelessness. I pray they will cast their burdens on You, Lord, releasing the weight of them, and You will sustain them. Hopelessness lies in wait to swallow up these little ones. I pray that whenever they are afraid or despair, they will cry out to You. I pray that their confidence and trust and reliance will be placed on You. You know their every sleepless night. You know each tear and heartache they hold. You are able to answer with Your promises. I am asking that You pull these children from the brink of despair, from the cliff edge of dread. May they see Your goodness. May they wait and hope for and expect You, the Living God, to draw close. Father, I know You are always watching each one of these children and are always thinking about them. Give me and their parents Your eyes and thoughts to meet their needs that they are too afraid to voice. Let us be the Hands and Feet and Heart of Jesus Christ to them. Father, give them understanding that death is not the final act. Teach them the hope they have of eternal life. You are the Resurrection and the Life. He who believes in You, though he may die, he will live. Death is swallowed up in victory. Give my grandchildren understanding of this truth and may it bring them comfort. Amen.

(Ps. 116: 15; Ps. 55: 22; 1 Peter 5: 7; John 11: 25–26;
1 Cor. 15: 13–14, 20, 22, 54, 57)

Father, as I sit quietly before You praying for my grandchildren, is there any word, Scripture, insight, or particular situation related to this topic which concerns my grandchildren that You want to bring to my heart? I surrender my thoughts to You and I commit to pray in obedience to what You reveal.

Word:

Date:

Parent's Loss of Job

Heavenly Father, regretfully my grandchildren's father(mother) is facing the loss of a job. I believe that the employer feels regret that this dismissal was necessary. I pray for the employer who made this decision. I extend peace to him in the Name of Jesus Christ. May my family refrain from harboring resentment, remembering that good things come from Your hand. Keep their focus on You and not bitterness toward the former employer.

My son (daughter-in-law) is hurt and worried. He is anxious to provide for his family. Help him overcome any feeling of panic, rejection, embarrassment, fear, or unfairness. He will need to remember that You have a plan and hope for him. My grandchildren are watching his reaction to this news. His response will model for them the authenticity of his faith in Your character. They will be given the opportunity to learn that everything that happens to believers is for their good and edification. I pray that my grandchildren will learn that You are the Lord; those who hope in You will not be disappointed. May they learn that everyone who trusts in You will never be put to shame. You will go before this family and will be with them; You will never leave or forsake them. You will be with them wherever they go. You are more than able to provide for their every need.

Father, as my son (daughter-in-law) begins a search for a new position, keep our family supportive and positive. We will see this as a blessing which opens new possibilities to this family's future. Please open the right doors which will lead him to employment that uses his skills and abilities in an excellent manner. May he see the deliverance You, Lord, will give. May he go out and face the world knowing You will be with him. In Jesus, he may approach You with freedom and confidence, making his requests known to You. May he seek You and not be discouraged. Use this job loss to teach my grandchildren how to cope with disappointments in a way that exhibits belief in Your goodness and brings glory to Your Name. Amen.

(Isaiah 49:23; Romans 10: 11; Deut. 31: 8; Joshua 1: 9;
2 Chronicles 20: 17; Ephesians 3: 13)

Father, as I sit quietly before You praying for my grandchildren, is there any word, Scripture, insight, or particular situation related to this topic which concerns my grandchildren that You want to bring to my heart? I surrender my thoughts to You and I commit to pray in obedience to what You reveal.

Word:

Date:

Divorce

O, Father, if there is any way to save my children's marriage, I implore You to intervene now! My children made vows of commitment and fidelity before You, and they must understand the gravity of this decision. You hate divorce, Lord God, and many lives are at stake. The law of the Old Testament permitted divorce because hearts were hard. But it was not Your plan from the beginning. May my children bend their knee and surrender their will to Yours. May the spirit of reconciliation dominate their lives and forgiveness be their stand.

If they move ahead with this decision to dissolve their marriage, I know my grandchildren will need You. You never abandon anyone who searches for You. My grandchildren will be like broken vessels. They will have heard rumors around them. They will be surrounded by fear. This will have a lasting effect on them. Be their Protector, mighty to save. They are trusting in You saying, "You are my God!" Their future is in your hands. Rescue them and let your favor shine on these children. In your unfailing love, save them from fear, despair, and resentment. Prevent their parents from forcing them to take sides. Remind their parents that angry words should not be spoken in front of their children.

The thought of suffering and homelessness is bitter beyond words. My grandchildren will never forget this awful time as they grieve over their loss. Yet they will dare to hope when they remember this: the unfailing love of the LORD never ends! By Your mercies they will be kept from complete destruction. Great is Your faithfulness; Your mercies begin afresh each day. May they say, "The LORD is my inheritance; therefore, I will hope in him!" For You, LORD, call them back from their grief—each one of them will feel deserted as though they were a young wife abandoned by her husband," says the Lord. "For a brief moment I abandoned you, but with great compassion I will take you back. In a moment of anger I turned my face away for a little while. But with everlasting love I will have compassion on you," says the LORD, our Redeemer. "You will be a joy to all generations, for I will make you so." Father, as their parents work through this crisis, they may neglect the needs of their children. Would You be their Father in this very difficult time. I will trust in You as Redeemer and King. Amen.

(Ps. 9: 10; Ps. 31: 12–17; Mal. 2: 16; Matt. 19: 8; Lam. 3: 19–24; Is. 54: 6–8; Is. 60: 15)

Death of a Baby or Child
"Chloe's Prayer"

Father, You see my heartache and take seriously my loss of a grandchild. You long to comfort a broken heart. For You have not despised or disdained the suffering of this afflicted one; You have not hidden Your face from me but have listened to my cry for help. In all my distress, You, too, are distressed; and the angel of Your Presence saves me. In Your love and mercy, You redeem me; You lift me up and carry me. You say that as a mother comforts her child, so will You comfort me and I will be consoled. When You see me, Your heart goes out to me and You say, "Do not cry."

(Ps. 22: 24; Isaiah 63: 9; Is. 66: 13; Luke 7: 13)

Father, I know that to You, every life is a complete life even though it may not look that way to me. You know exactly how long each person will live. Some miscarry and some live more than a century. But every life is a complete life. Whether a life spans decades or blooms and fades in minutes, it is a complete life. You make no mistakes.

O, LORD, You have searched my grandchild thoroughly and have known her . . . Where could she go from Your Spirit or where could she flee from Your Presence? If she ascends up to heaven, You are there; If she makes her bed in the place of the dead, behold You are there . . . Her frame was not hidden from You when she was being formed in secret and intricately and curiously wrought in the depths of the earth. Your eyes saw her unformed substance, and in Your

book all the days of her life were written before they ever took shape,
when as yet there was not one of them. (Psalm 139)

Show me, O LORD, my life's end and the number of my days; let me
know how fleeting is my life. You have made my days a mere hand-
breadth; the span of my years is as nothing before You. Each man's
life is but a breath. (Ps. 39: 4–5 NIV)

Father, You love little children and welcome them into Your Kingdom. This baby girl is in the Presence of God and knows more about Him than I do. She is rejoicing and filled with delight in her life with Christ. This baby is thoroughly conscious, perfect, and forever in the Presence of Jesus. I will see this child again in heaven. Jesus said, "Let the little children come to Me and do not hinder them, for the Kingdom of heaven belongs to such as these." You tend Your flock like a shepherd: You gather the lambs in Your arms and carry them close to Your heart; You gently lead those that have young. The promise of the Holy Spirit is to me and for me and my children, and to and for all that are far away ~ for all whom the Lord our God will call. In the Father's house are many rooms; if it were not so, Jesus would have told me. Jesus went to prepare a place for me and my grandchildren. I know that my Redeemer lives and that in the end He will stand upon the earth. And after my flesh has been destroyed, yet I will see God. I myself will see Him with my own eyes. I and not another. How my heart yearns within me!

(Matt 19: 14 NIV; Is. 40: 11; Acts 2: 39; John 14:2;
Job 19: 25–27 NIV)

You have purposes that I cannot understand. Your thoughts are not my thoughts, neither are Your ways my ways. As the heavens are higher than the earth, so are Your ways higher than my ways and Your thoughts higher than my thoughts. The secret things belong to the Lord my God, but the things revealed belong to me and my children forever.

(Is. 55:8–9; Deut. 29:29)

Incline Your ear, O LORD, and answer me, for I am poor in spirit, needy and desiring. Preserve my life; save Your servant for I trust in You. Be merciful and gracious to me for to You I cry all day long. Make me rejoice, O LORD, for to You do I lift my heart. For You are good and ready to forgive; and You are abundant in mercy and loving-kindness to all who call upon You. Give ear, O LORD, to my prayers; and listen to the cry of my supplications. In the day of my troubles I will call upon You, for You will answer me. Amen.

(Psalm 86 TAB)

O merciful Father, Your angels behold the face of Your little ones in heaven. May I steadfastly believe that my grandchild, Your precious baby, has been taken into the safekeeping of Your eternal love, through Jesus Christ, my Lord. Amen.

Almighty and Merciful God Who grants to Your children an abundant and welcoming entrance into Your Kingdom; behold this baby's innocence and perfect faith. And at length, at the end of my days, I pray a fullest joy as I re-unite with her in Your Presence. Amen.

In sure and certain hope of the Resurrection, we commit the

body of this child to the ground. The Lord bless her and keep her. The Lord make His Face shine upon her and be gracious to her. The LORD lift up His countenance upon her and give her peace now and evermore. Amen.

Behold, this precious baby is before the Throne of God! She will serve Him day and night in His temple: and He that sits on the Throne will dwell among His people. This baby will never hunger or thirst. Nor will the sun light on her, nor any heat nor darkness. For the Lamb will feed her and will lead her into living fountains of water: and You, God, will wipe away every tear from her eyes. Amen.

Almighty God, Father of all mercy and giver of all comfort, deal graciously with us who mourn. Let us know the consolation of Your love at this deeply sorrowful time.

Jesus said, "You now have sorrow. But I will see you again, and your hearts will rejoice. And your joy - no man can take from you."

"Surely goodness and mercy will follow me all the days of my life and I will dwell in the House of the Lord forever." Amen.

Adapted from the Book of Common Prayer

- Holidays -

Valentine's Day

Heavenly Father, on this day that celebrates love, I thank You that Your love is being poured forth into the hearts of my grandchildren by the Holy Spirit Who has been given to them. May they keep and treasure Your Word. Love for You is being perfected and completed in these children, and perfect love casts out fear. Father, I believe in faith that each of my grandchildren will be Your children, called by Your Name, and I pray that they will commit to walk in divine love. May they endure long; may they be patient and kind. I pray they will not be envious nor will they boil over with jealousy. May they not be boastful nor vainglorious, and may they not display themselves haughtily. May my grandchildren not be rude and unmannerly, nor act unbecomingly, nor insist on their own rights or their own way. I pray in faith that my grandchildren will not be self-seeking, touchy, fretful, or resentful. May they take no account of evil done to them and pay no attention to suffered wrongs. May they not rejoice in injustice and unrighteousness, but rejoice when right and truth prevail. I pray that my grandchildren will bear up under anything and everything that comes. May they be ready to believe the best of others. Their hopes will be fadeless under all circumstances, for this pleases You. May they endure everything without weakening because Your love which resides in them never fails. Father, I pray that my grandchildren will bless and pray for those who persecute them ~ who are cruel in their attitudes toward my grandchildren. Their love will then abound more and more in knowledge and all judgment. My grandchildren will approve things that are excellent. They will be sincere and without offense until the day of Christ. They will be filled with the fruits of righteousness. May my grandchildren be rooted deep in love and founded securely on love, knowing that You are on their side and nothing is able to separate them from Your love which is in Christ Jesus, their Lord. I thank You, Lord God, for Your love for my grandchildren in the precious Name of Jesus. Amen.

(1 Cor. 13; 1 Cor. 7:10)

Father, as I sit quietly before You praying for my grandchildren, is there any word, Scripture, insight, or particular situation related to this topic on love which concerns my grandchildren that You want to bring to my heart? I surrender my thoughts to You and I commit to pray in obedience to what You reveal.

Word:

Date:

Easter

This is the most joyous season of the entire year, because it represents that Christ, the Paschal Lamb, has been sacrificed for all who call on the Name of Jesus. The Lamb who was slain has risen. O Risen Jesus, You have made my grandchildren worthy to share in the joy of Your Resurrection. You have made my grandchildren for Yourself, and they cannot live without You. You are the only One who can satisfy their hearts. O what exceeding mercy! What favor is beyond deserving! May they rejoice, because You, Lord, find Your delight in them. May all things on earth rejoice in the greatness of our God. May my grandchildren desire neither the world nor anything that is worldly; may nothing give them pleasure but You. Everything else will seem a heavy cross.

O God, my grandchildren are not afraid, and with good reason. Blessed may You be forever! For though they have forsaken You, You have not forsaken them. You raise them up again and again by continually giving them Your hand. You have remembered their great misery, O Lord, and You look upon their weakness, since You know all things. You are the Resurrection and the Life. You ascended to heaven in the triumph of Your glory and You are seated at the right hand of the Father; You Who are all-powerful, raise my grandchildren up to You.

Jesus, Your Cross is my grandchildren's gateway into Your Life. Your Resurrection means that You have the power to convey Your Life to them. When they were born again, they received the very life of the Risen Lord. Your Resurrection destiny ~ Your foreordained purpose ~ was to bring "many sons to glory." One day they will have a body like Your glorious body, but they can know now the power and effectiveness of Your Resurrection and can walk in newness of life. In the Name of Jesus, Amen.

(Heb. 2: 10; Phil. 3: 10)

Father, as I sit quietly before You praying for my grandchildren, is there any word, Scripture, insight, or particular situation related to Easter and the Resurrection that You want to bring to my heart? I surrender my thoughts to You and I commit to pray in obedience to what You reveal.

Word:

Date:

Fourth of July

Heavenly Father, I praise You as the Author of all liberty. I do not take lightly what You have done in and for our nation. I desire to see our nation restored to Godly integrity and excellence. I appreciate the deep privilege of living in freedom and having the privilege of worshipping You without restraint. I pray that my grandchildren will see the opportunity of living in a free nation as a gift from Your Hand. May there arise such a force of righteousness in this nation that every realm and every level of government will submit its power and influence under the Mighty Hand of God. May my grandchildren be a part of the Christian community and voice of our nation that serve as standard bearers of Light and Truth who profoundly affect the morality of our nation. May I as a grandparent teach my grandchildren the virtue of being good citizens ~ to live not only for the good of the individual but the good of others as well. Bless the United States of America. In Jesus' Name, I pray. Amen.

Father, as I sit quietly before You praying for my grandchildren, is there any word, Scripture, insight, or particular situation related to this topic which concerns my grandchildren that You want to bring to my heart? I surrender my thoughts to You and I commit to pray in obedience to what You reveal.

Word:

Date:

Halloween

Father, even I am lured by the store displays of cute goblins and ghouls, carved pumpkins and "trick or treat" paraphernalia. How much more so my grandchildren, who enjoy playing dress-up and donning costumes. I have justified celebrating the season by giving Halloween a harvest theme. Forgive me, Father, for indulging in any way the promotion of a festival that glorifies our enemy. You died on a Cross to rescue me from his temptations which lead to death. I was a person living in darkness until You revealed to me a great light; I was living in the land of the shadow of death when a light dawned. Jesus said, "I am the light of the world. Whoever follows Me will never walk in darkness, but will have the light of life." And, "I have come into the world as a light, so that no one who believes in Me should stay in darkness." Paul wrote, "You are all sons of the light and sons of the day. You do not belong to the night or to the darkness." Peter said, "But you are a chosen people, a royal priesthood, a holy nation, a people belonging to God, that you may declare the praises of Him who called you out of darkness into His wonderful light."

Father, I do not want to judge people who enjoy Halloween. The god of this age has blinded the minds of unbelievers so that they cannot see the light of the gospel of the glory of Christ, who is the image of God. The light shines in the darkness, but the darkness has not understood it. Allow me to use Halloween to teach my grandchildren that they have received a rich inheritance. We are no longer a people who imitate witches and ghosts, monsters and demons. We worship Jesus, the Light of the World. At this season, may my grandchildren worship Him all the more as they glory in His goodness to them. May my family celebrate the harvest and the splendor of the fall season.

Our pumpkins and leaves and berries and corn stalks will remind us that Jesus is Lord of every season. In His Name, I pray. Amen.

(Matt. 4: 16; John 1: 5 NIV; John 8: 12; John 12: 46,
2 Cor. 4: 4 NIV; 1 Thess. 5: 5 NIV; 1 Peter 2: 9 NIV)

Father, as I sit quietly before You praying for my grandchildren, is there any word, Scripture, insight, or particular situation related to this topic which concerns my grandchildren that You want to bring to my heart? I surrender my thoughts to You and I commit to pray in obedience to what You reveal.

Word:

Date:

Thanksgiving Day Prayer

Heavenly Father, in this season of thankfulness, I reflect on the gift of Your Son sent into this world. I thank You that You brought my grandchildren into the world, entrusted into my loving care. Help me to remember that I am to love and nurture these little ones in order that they may attain to that full stature intended for them in Your eternal kingdom. This Thanksgiving I give You hearty thanks and praise for the seedtime and harvest, for the increase of the ground and the gathering in of its fruits. I thank You that You Who supply seed to the sower and bread for food will also supply and increase the store of seed my grandchildren have sown and will enlarge the harvest of their righteousness. May they not become weary in doing good, for at the appointed season they will reap a harvest if they do not give up. May each moment with my grandchildren be a time of planting spiritual seeds. May I bless them in such a way that they grow in Your Spirit and produce good fruit. And may I live to see the harvest of their souls for Your glory. I pray this in the Name of Your Son. Amen.

(Ps. 69: 30; Ps. 95: 2; Ps. 100:4, 2 Cor. 9: 10; Gal. 6: 9)

Father, as I sit quietly before You praying for my grandchildren, is there any word, Scripture, insight, or particular situation related to this topic which concerns my grandchildren that You want to bring to my heart? I surrender my thoughts to You and I commit to pray in obedience to what You reveal.

Word:

Date:

Pre-Christmas Prayer

Heavenly Father, I pray for my grandchildren during this busy week leading up to Christmas. My prayer is that in the midst of fun-filled activities celebrating this holiday season, Your Holy Spirit will break through and teach my grandchildren the glorious truth of the birth of a Savior. Though many of my grandchildren are still infants and toddlers, I ask that You prepare their hearts for that day when they will personally know Jesus as Immanuel, God with us. Please, Lord God, arrange those moments that their parents can teach and demonstrate by their lives the profound promises that Christmas holds. May my grandchildren reverently bow before the holy Child Whose innocence restored to mankind its ancient glory; and I pray that He may be formed in my grandchildren, the hope of glory. In Jesus' Name, I pray. Amen.

Father, as I sit quietly before You praying for my grandchildren, is there any word, Scripture, insight, or particular situation related to Christmas which concerns my grandchildren that You want to bring to my heart? I surrender my thoughts to You and I commit to pray in obedience to what You reveal.

Word:

Date:

January First

Heavenly Father, I know that time passes and does not return. I acknowledge that You have assigned to me a definite time in which to fulfill Your divine plan for my soul; I have only this time and will have no more. My life is made up of this continual, uninterrupted flow of time which never returns. In eternity, on the contrary, time will be no more; I will be established forever.

O, LORD, I look back on the year just passed, a year given by Your divine Providence in which to increase my love of You and to nurture and cherish my grandchildren, gifts from Your hand. In some ways I can only grieve and say to You, how little I have loved You, O God! How badly I have often spent my time! How many opportunities I ignored that would have strengthened my grandchildren's walk in the faith. O God of mercy, how powerful You are. In a moment, You can turn loss to gain. Nothing is impossible for You Who can do all things. Restore the time and opportunities I have lost, granting me Your grace to do Your bidding in this coming year. You know that I will try to avoid making sacrifices, for my nature seeks what is easiest, what is the least tiring, what is safe, and what is comfortable. I soon fall into negligence, selfishness, and laziness. In reality, I am still tenacious, obstinate and hard to bend, too firm in my shortsightedness. This new year, I ask that You would continue to make me more supple and submissive to You. Strengthen me in my heart so that I may be enabled to conquer every weakness, every spiritual vacillation and hesitation, especially when You call me to overcome difficulties and face sacrifice. May there be no distinction between Your will and mine. May there be perfect union and perfect peace.

Help me this coming year, O LORD, and strengthen my love by Your almighty power. Grant, O GOD, that I do whatever You ask with all the love possible. Change me and use me in impacting the lives of my grandchildren as I yield to Your amazing love.

O Lord, give my grandchildren Your peace in this new year; let it establish Your kingdom in them and make them a praise of Your glory. Let my grandchildren be called oaks of righteousness, the planting of the Lord, for the display of Your splendor.

How much You have given me! Everlasting praise be to the Father, Son, and Holy Spirit. Amen.

(Ps. 139; Ps. 39: 4–5; Is. 61: 3)

"Let us not weary in doing good, for at the proper time, we will reap a harvest if we do not give up. Therefore, while we have the time, let us do good to all people, especially to those who belong to the family of believers." Gal. 6:9–10 NIV

Father, as I sit quietly before You praying for my grandchildren, is there any word, Scripture, insight, or particular situation related to the beginning of this new year which concerns my grandchildren that You want to bring to my heart? I surrender my thoughts to You and I commit to pray in obedience to what You reveal.

Word:

Date:

Prayers for Character
Development

Belief

Heavenly Father, above all things I pray that my grandchildren will believe in You, the Lord their God, and they will be established. I pray that they will believe in Your Son, because this is Your power at work for the salvation of everyone who believes. In order for Your work to take hold, my grandchildren must be people of faith. To walk in faith, they will need to look beyond this world to an unseen realm. You will help them to understand that this world, during the successive ages, was framed and fashioned, put in order, and equipped for its intended purpose by the Word of Your mouth. I thank You that You desire to open their minds and allow them to see that this world was not made from things which are visible. May my grandchildren turn away from all that will distract, and instead turn to Jesus, Who is the Leader and the Source of their faith. I can rest in the knowledge that as Jesus gives the first incentive for their belief, He is also the Finisher of their faith, bringing it to maturity and perfection. May my grandchildren have an absolute trust and confidence in Your power, wisdom, and goodness. From their childhood, will You inspire their parents, teachers, and mentors, and give them divine knowledge of Your sacred Writings, which are intended to instruct them. May my grandchildren be granted understanding of the salvation which comes through faith in Jesus, for if they do not stand firm in their faith, they will not stand at all. In Jesus' Name, I pray. Amen.

(Rom. 1:16; Heb. 11:3; Heb. 12: 2; Is. 7: 9; 2 Tim. 3: 15; 2 Tim. 4: 7)

Father, as I sit quietly before You praying for my grandchildren, is there any word, Scripture, insight, or particular situation related to belief which concerns my grandchildren that You want to bring to my heart? I surrender my thoughts to You and I commit to pray in obedience to what You reveal.

Word:

Date:

Boldness

Almighty Father, reveal Yourself in such a powerful way to my grandchildren and to their generation that in their lifetimes, more attention and honor and glory will be ascribed to You than at any other time in history. Give this generation of children hearts like David, so that their faith will enable them to conquer the Goliaths they face. May they say to anyone who defies and ridicules the Lord God: *"You come against me with sword and spear and javelin, but I come against you in the name of the LORD Almighty . . . whom you have defied. This day the LORD will defeat you and the whole world will know that there is only One True God. All those gathered here will know that it is not by sword or spear that the LORD saves; for the battle is the LORD's, and He will give all of you into our hands."* May my grandchildren know that their Redeemer, their Defender, lives; and that in the end He will stand upon the earth. May they know that their Defender is strong; He will take up their case. May they be uncompromisingly righteous and bold as lions. May they be fearless in their defense of the Gospel. In Jesus' Name. Amen.

(1 Sam. 17:25–51; Job 19:25; Prov. 23: 11; Prov. 28: 1; Joshua 1: 7)

Father, as I sit quietly before You praying for my grandchildren, is there any word, Scripture, insight, or particular situation related to boldness which concerns my grandchildren that You want to bring to my heart? I surrender my thoughts to You and I commit to pray in obedience to what You reveal.

Word:

Date:

Contentment

Heavenly Father, through the power of Your perfect and unerring Word, I call upon You to replace any dissatisfaction in my grandchildren's lives with contentment, joy, hope, and happiness. I trust in Your Word which says that they will be satisfied and they will have every good thing. Through my faith and the authority of Your Word, I now pray that as my grandchildren grow to maturity, they will choose to throw off their old selfish nature, which is full of worldly passions and deception. I pray they will yield their thoughts to the Lord Jesus Christ so that they will no longer think of ways to indulge their evil desires. May they put off envy, covetousness, and discontent, for You tell us to guard ourselves and keep free from greedy longing. Your Word says that a man's life does not consist in his possessions, even when they overflow with abundance beyond his needs. It is written that our character and moral disposition should be free from love of money, greed, avarice, lust, and craving for earthly possessions. We should be satisfied with our present circumstances and with what we have; for You will not in any way fail us, nor give us up, nor leave us without support. You will not in any degree leave us helpless, nor forsake, nor relax Your hold on us. Father, I pray that my grandchildren will trust in this truth and put on contentment, for true religion with contentment is great wealth. After all, we brought nothing with us when we came into the world, and we certainly cannot carry anything with us when we die. Therefore, if my grandchildren have enough food and clothing, let them be content. Those who long to be rich fall into temptation and are trapped by many foolish and harmful desires that plunge them into ruin and destruction. Father, keep my grandchildren from envying not only material goods, but others' talents, gifts, positions, family, looks - all the intangibles that man inwardly measures. Let them not become conceited or competitive; nor challenge, provoke or irritate others; nor envy what others have. I pray my grandchildren will seek You, Lord, and in You they will be satisfied and not lack any good thing. In Jesus' Name. Amen.

(Eph. 4: 22; Romans 13: 14; Luke 12:15; Heb. 13: 5;
1 Tim. 6: 6–9; Gal. 5: 26)

Father, as I sit quietly before You praying for my grandchildren, is there any word, Scripture, insight, or particular situation related to contentment or envy which concerns my grandchildren that You want to bring to my heart? I surrender my thoughts to You and I commit to pray in obedience to what You reveal.

Word:

Date:

Courage

Lord, make my grandchildren strong; fill them with courage for every task. You have already equipped them with everything they need to fulfill Your plans for them. Teach them to rely on You, not on their own abilities, and they will be able to do all things through Jesus Who brings them strength. May they fear nothing, nor be dismayed; for You, Lord, are with them. I pray that my grandchildren will be anxious for nothing, but will in all things make their request known to You with thanksgiving, through prayer and supplication. I pray that You, the eternal God, are my grandchildren's refuge, and You will thrust out the enemy from before them. May they be of good courage as You strengthen their hearts, for their hope is in You, Lord. When they pass through the waters, You will be with them; and through the rivers, they will not overflow them. When they walk through the fire, they will not be burned, nor will the flame scorch them. For You are the Lord their God. You will not fail nor forsake them while they work to complete the service of the house of the Lord. Amen.

(Joshua 1: 9, 17–18; Phil. 4: 13; Deut. 33: 27; Ps. 31: 24;
Phil 4: 6; Is. 43: 2–3; 1 Chron 28: 20)

Father, as I sit quietly before You praying for my grandchildren, is there any word, Scripture, insight, or particular situation related to courage which concerns my grandchildren that You want to bring to my heart? I surrender my thoughts to You and I commit to pray in obedience to what You reveal.

Word:

Date:

Discernment

Heavenly Father, Almighty God, this is my prayer: that my grandchildren will grow in spiritual knowledge and understanding, in equal measure with the love which overflows in their hearts. Father, give my grandchildren wise and discerning hearts, such that there will never have been, nor ever will be, anyone like them. As the heart of the discerning acquires knowledge and the ears of the wise seek it out, so may it be for my grandchildren. I pray they will discern what matters to You, so that they may live pure and blameless lives until Christ returns. May they preserve sound judgment and not let it out of their sight. Give them discernment that they may understand Your statutes. Let them discern for themselves what is right; let them learn together what is good. May they always be filled with the fruit of their salvation—those good things that are produced in their life by Jesus Christ—for this will bring glory and praise to You. You, Lord God, change times and seasons; You set up kings and depose them. You give wisdom to the wise and knowledge to the discerning. I pray that my grandchildren will receive these gifts and will not be like the man without the Spirit who does not accept the things that come from the Spirit of God. To him, spiritual things are foolishness. Instead, because the things of the Spirit are discerned spiritually, I pray that my grandchildren, filled with Your Spirit, will know and understand them. Your Word says that wisdom reposes in the hearts of the discerning. May this be Your blessing for my grandchildren. In Jesus' Name, I pray. Amen.

(Phil 1: 9–11; 1 Kings 3: 12; Job 34: 4; Ps. 119: 125; Prov. 3: 21; Prov. 14: 33; Prov. 15: 14; Prov 18: 15; Dan. 2: 21; 1 Cor. 2: 14)

Father, as I sit quietly before You praying for my grandchildren, is there any word, Scripture, insight, or particular situation regarding discernment which concerns my grandchildren that You want to bring to my heart? I surrender my thoughts to You and I commit to pray in obedience to what You reveal.

Word:

Date:

Faith

Heavenly Father, O, that my grandchildren would be counted among those who walk by faith and not by sight, for without faith, it is impossible to please You. You commended the ancient fathers in days of old because of their faith. Abraham believed You and his faith was credited as righteousness. Barnabas was full of the Holy Spirit and strong in faith. When Jesus touched the eyes of the blind man, He said, "According to your faith and trust in the power invested in Me, it will be done to you." Depth of faith leads to holy devotion and earnest piety. Please increase the faith of my grandchildren. Let their faith come by hearing what is told ~ the preaching of the message that comes from the lips of Christ the Messiah Himself. May my grandchildren have a pure heart, a good conscience, and sincere faith. May they always remember that faith is the substance of things hoped for and the evidence of things not seen.

Faith is not revealed to the senses, but is rooted deep in the heart, and whatever is not from faith is sin. My grandchildren's faith will give them the inclination and the power to do anything in Your service. Faith without works is dead; if it does not have works, deeds, and actions of obedience to back it up, by itself it is destitute of power. I pray that their faith remembers the promise: *"Your castles and strongholds shall have bars of iron and bronze, and so will your strength, your rest, and your security equal your days"*—so boldly they will venture. Help them take up the covering shield of saving faith, upon which they can quench all the flaming missiles of the wicked one. They belong to the day; therefore, may they be sober and put on the breastplate of faith and love. May they realize that to come to You, they must believe that You are, and that You reward those who diligently seek You. As they believe, establish them. Help them remain steadfast to Your prophets, so that they will prosper. I pray my grandchildren will fight the good, worthy, honorable, and noble fight, and will finish the race, and will keep and firmly hold the faith. For there are three things that will endure—faith, hope, and love. Having been justified by faith, they will have peace with You. In Jesus' Name, I pray. Amen.

(2 Cor. 5:7; 1 Tim. 1: 5; Heb. 11: 1; Matt. 9: 29;
Rom. 5: 1, 10: 17; Rom. 10: 17; 1 Tim. 1: 5; Heb. 11: 1, 6;
James 2: 17; Eph. 6: 16; 1 Thess. 5: 8; Gen. 15: 6;
Romans 4: 9; Deut. 33: 25; 2 Chron 20:20;
1 Cor. 13: 13; Heb. 11: 1; 2 Tim. 4:7))

Father, as I sit quietly before You praying for my grandchildren, is there any word, Scripture, insight, or particular situation related to my grandchildren's faith that You want to bring to my heart? I surrender my thoughts to You and I commit to pray in obedience to what You reveal.

Word:

Date:

Faithfulness

Lord God, love and faithfulness meet together; righteousness and peace kiss each other. Let mercy and faithfulness never leave my grandchildren. Bind these twin virtues around their necks and write them on the tablet of their hearts. May they be clothed as Your own chosen ones, purified and holy and well-beloved by You. May their actions be marked by tenderhearted pity and mercy, kind feeling, gentle ways, and patience which is tireless and long-suffering, and which has the power to endure whatever comes with good temper. May my grandchildren exhibit Your character. May they be compassionate and gracious, slow to anger, abounding in love and faithfulness. Father, may my grandchildren fear the LORD and serve You with all faithfulness. May they throw away the gods and idols their forefathers worshiped, and serve only the LORD. May they be enthroned in Your presence forever. Appoint Your love and faithfulness to protect them. For great is Your love, reaching to the heavens; Your faithfulness reaches to the skies. I will praise You with the harp for Your faithfulness toward my grandchildren, O God; I will sing praise to You with the lyre, O Holy One of Israel. In Jesus' Name, I pray. Amen.

(Ps. 85: 10; Prov. 3:3; Col. 3: 12; Ex. 34:6; Joshua 24: 14;
Ps. 61: 7; Ps. 57:10; Ps. 71: 22 NIV)

Father, as I sit quietly before You praying for my grandchildren, is there any word, Scripture, insight, or particular situation related to this topic on faithfulness which concern my grandchildren that You want to bring to my heart? I surrender my thoughts to You and I commit to pray in obedience to what You reveal.

Word:

Date:

Forgiveness

Heavenly Father, I know my grandchildren will be hurt by others. I pray for forgiveness for those who hurt them or speak unkind words about them. Teach my grandchildren to walk in forgiveness, and to love even their enemies so that they may be Your sons and daughters. For You cause the sun to rise on both evil and good, and You send rain on the righteous and the unrighteous. If my grandchildren love only those who love them, what reward will they get? And if they greet only their brothers and friends, what are they doing that unbelievers do not? They are called to reach out to all people, even those who are difficult or might bring them harm. This is Your sacred work which sanctifies and transforms. Therefore, I thank You that they can rejoice in trials and struggles because these tests of faith develop character and perseverance. Perseverance must finish its work so that they will be made mature and complete, not lacking anything in their character. With that in mind, I will not become embittered when my grandchildren are hurt, but rather will know You are at work in their lives. I pray that their temporary wounding will develop Godly character. I pray that my grandchildren will be holy, as their heavenly Father is holy. May they become people who are not easily offended and who forgive readily. Teach them to model themselves after Your Son Who was placed on a Cross and spoke forgiveness to a lost world. May they walk in forgiveness. In Christ's Name, Amen.

(Matt. 5:43–48; James 1:2–4)

Father, as I sit quietly before You praying for my grandchildren, is there any word, Scripture, insight, or particular situation related to forgiveness which concerns my grandchildren that You want to bring to my heart? I surrender my thoughts to You and I commit to pray in obedience to what You reveal.

Word:

Date:

Generosity

Lord God, I pray for my precious grandchildren. Grant that they may become generous people, always willing to share. By doing this they will store up for themselves the riches that endure forever, and so take hold of the life that is really life. May they give generously without a grudging heart. Then You, the LORD their God, will bless them in all their work and in everything they put their hand to. You have commanded us to be openhanded toward our brothers and toward the poor and needy in the land. You have said that a generous man will prosper; that he who refreshes others will himself be refreshed. May my grandchildren learn and remember this: whoever sows sparingly will also reap sparingly, and whoever sows generously will also reap generously. May they be made rich in every way so that they can be generous on every occasion. May their generosity to others result in others giving thanksgiving to You, God. May I teach my grandchildren by example the spiritual benefits that come from generosity. In Jesus' Name, I pray. Amen.

(1 Tim. 6: 18–19; Deut. 15: 10; Prov. 11: 25; 2 Cor. 9: 6, 11)

Father, as I sit quietly before You praying for my grandchildren, is there any word, Scripture, insight, or particular situation related to generosity which concerns my grandchildren that You want to bring to my heart? I surrender my thoughts to You and I commit to pray in obedience to what You reveal.

Word:

Date:

Hope

Heavenly Father, my grandchildren's lives are just beginning, and as they grow, You will provide many opportunities for them. I give thanks that You are a God of hope. My grandchildren will hold on to particular dreams and hopes You have planted in them for their personal lives and for our corporate lives within the Body of Christ. These visions can energize us, but sometimes we think our personal dreams are impossible to reach. My grandchildren will need the truth, not fantasy, so that when You place hope in them, it will be worth the struggle to follow after their dreams. I pray that they will ask for Your direction. I ask You to show them what they do not see, to redirect them if there are other ways to go, to answer if they have missed anything, and to reveal to them what You are doing and what doors You are opening for them.

I pray that my grandchildren will let go of specific hopes and expectations if this is Your will. However, keep them from giving up prematurely. When grace is hidden from them, help them to wait expectantly for You to show Your Hand mightily. May their temporary disappointments not cause crises of faith, but provide opportunities to learn trust. They will need a basis for the hope to which they cling. Build faith in their inner man. When they claim a particular dream in faith, may they know they will always face a great challenge. Indeed, this is why they will need great hope, and the energy and determination which hope provides.

May they walk in faith forever; but, Father, I ask that You also give my grandchildren hope for the things You see for them. Keep them on Your path for their future. I claim for my grandchildren

Your promises, that *"Those who wait on the Lord will find new strength,"* and *"those who trust in You will never be put to shame."* In Jesus' Name, I pray. Amen.

(Ps. 71: 1 NIV; Isaiah 40:31 NIV)

Father, as I sit quietly before You praying for my grandchildren, is there any word, Scripture, insight, or particular situation related to hope which concerns my grandchildren that You want to bring to my heart? I surrender my thoughts to You and I commit to pray in obedience to what You reveal.

Word:

Date:

Humility

Heavenly Father, because my grandchildren are still young, they will naturally want others to see to their own needs and wants. As they journey to adulthood, I ask for Your Holy Spirit to prompt them towards another way of living. May they live selflessly. Instead of demanding and insisting, may they extend and give of themselves. May my grandchildren do nothing from selfish motives, or for unworthy ends. Prevent their actions from being prompted by conceit and empty arrogance. Instead, in the true spirit of humility and lowliness of mind, let each of them regard others first. May they think more highly of others than they do of themselves. May they be people who are concerned not merely for their own interests, but also for the interests of others.

Let this same attitude and purpose and humble mind that was in Christ Jesus be in each of my grandchildren. May they look to Jesus as their example of true humility. Jesus, being essentially one with You, and in the divine form, possessed the fullness of Your attributes. Yet, He did not think this equality with You as a thing to be eagerly grasped, but He stripped Himself of all divine privileges and heavenly glory, and assumed the guise of a servant. He became like man and was born a human being. And after He had appeared in human form, He abased and humbled Himself still further and carried His obedience to the extreme of death, even the death of the cross! Therefore, because He stooped so low, You, Lord God, have highly exalted Him and have freely bestowed on Him the Name that is above every name. All men will bow down to Him.

Bring my grandchildren to that place of true humility. At the

Name of Jesus, may my grandchildren bow their knees and confess with their mouths frankly and openly and acknowledge that Jesus Christ is Lord. May they, too, serve others at great sacrifice to themselves. To Your honor and to Your glory, God my Father, I pray. Amen.

(Phil 2: 3–13)

Father, as I sit quietly before You praying for my grandchildren, is there any word, Scripture, insight, or particular situation related to humility which concerns my grandchildren that You want to bring to my heart? I surrender my thoughts to You and I commit to pray in obedience to what You reveal.

Word:

Date:

Inscribed Heart

Father, by the enlightenment of Your Holy Spirit, help me to open the mystery of Your Word to my grandchildren. Your Scriptures contain Truth that cannot be found in any other writings. Your thoughts lie far beyond our thoughts. What the world regards as wisdom, You regard as foolishness. How I look forward to my grandchildren discovering and delighting in the complexities of Your ways and the glorious paradoxes of Your Word. Teach my grandchildren to give gifts and perform acts of charity in secret, and You Father, Who know all secrets, will reward them. Lead them in praying by themselves, going away to a quiet place to be with You alone. May they shut the door, and pray to You in secret; then You will reward them with Your comforting Presence and revelation. May my grandchildren learn the value of loving their enemies, as well as those people they enjoy. May they submit to those in authority over them and understand that protection comes as a result. May they humble themselves and so be lifted up by You. May they learn that if they try to keep their life for themselves, they will lose it, but if they give up their life for Jesus, they will find true life. May they be kind and do good so that others benefit from their favors. May they grow to be people who give expecting and hoping for nothing in return, but also considering nothing as lost and despairing of no one. For if they help those who cannot pay them in kind, they will be lending to You—and You will repay them. Thank you, Father, that as I teach my grandchildren the standards to which You beckon us, You will inscribe Your laws upon the hearts of these little ones and imprint them on their minds, on their inmost thoughts and understanding.

According to Your Word, may they purpose to do things in secret which only Your eyes will see, and wait for their heavenly reward, to be able to stand in Your Presence. Amen.

(Is. 55: 8; Matt.6: 1–6; Luke 6: 27, Luke 6: 35; Jer. 31: 33;
Luke 9: 24)

Father, as I sit quietly before You praying for my grandchildren, is there any word, Scripture, insight, or particular situation related to Your inscribing Your Word on my grandchildren's hearts that You want to bring to my mind? I surrender my thoughts to You and I commit to pray in obedience to what You reveal.

Word:

Date:

Integrity

Heavenly Father, I pray for the men and women my grandchildren will become. I ask for Your Spirit to develop my grandchildren into people of integrity all their lives. May integrity and honesty be their virtue. I know, Lord God, that You test the heart and are pleased with honor and steadfastness. May my grandchildren give willingly and with honest intent. The person of integrity walks securely, but he who takes crooked paths will be found out. May my grandchildren walk securely. May they repay no one with evil for evil, but take thought for what is honest and proper and noble, aiming to be above reproach in the sight of everyone. May they always take thought beforehand and aim to be honest and absolutely above suspicion, not only in Your sight, but also in the sight of men. And may they learn to apply themselves to good deeds, honest labor, and honorable employment, so that they may be able to meet necessary demands whenever the occasion may require. Keep them from living idle, uncultivated, and unfruitful lives. I pray this in Your Son's Name. Amen.

(Ps. 25: 21; 1 Chron 29:17; Prov. 10: 9; Rom. 12:17; 2 Cor 8: 21; Titus 3: 14)

Father, as I sit quietly before You praying for my grandchildren, is there any word, Scripture, insight, or particular situation related to this topic on integrity which concerns my grandchildren that You want to bring to my heart? I surrender my thoughts to You and I commit to pray in obedience to what You reveal.

Word:

Date:

Intimacy

Almighty Father, true believers worship You with reverence and fear. Some devote time in studying Your ways and Your truths, practicing the disciplines of the faith. Fewer still seek an intimate relationship and friendship with You. Your Word reveals that Adam walked closely with You in the garden before he was driven out. Enoch walked in habitual fellowship with You. The Word says, *"and then he was not, for God took him home with Him."* Enoch was so close to You that one day he simply no longer was; he was eternally with You. Abraham knew You so intimately that You called him Your friend. And what friendship Moses had with You, Lord! You spoke with him face to face, clearly and not in riddles. Moses was a man who saw Your form. Jesus told His disciples that He no longer called them servants; instead, He called them friends, for everything He learned from the Father, He made known to them. May my grandchildren be known to You as Your friends!

Jesus taught His disciples by example that they must have solitary times and places to be alone with You. May You help my grandchildren consistently choose a secret time to place themselves in Your heavenly Presence for intimate worship and conversation. May they learn that You are waiting there and will be found by them. May they approach You, Lord, as Your acknowledged friends, with minds and lives deeply connected to Your heart. Your friendship will give them the liberty to say, *"I have a Friend to Whom I can go even in my darkest moments. He knows me. My voice will be heard. I have a Friend Who will help me. I can trust Him in the face of crushing disappointment."* May my grandchildren know living and direct fellowship with You.

It is Your will that Your Name should be glorified in and through these children, these children who trust You as their close and intimate Friend. Let this desire of Yours be their confidence. Let their intimacy with You give them certainty in their lives, that whatever comes, You will forever be their Lord and their Friend. Amen.

(Gen. 5: 21–24; James 2: 23; Num. 12: 8, Deut. 34: 10;
2 Chron. 20: 7; John 15: 15)

Father, as I sit quietly before You praying for my grandchildren, is there any word, Scripture, insight, or particular situation concerning intimacy that You want to bring to my heart? I surrender my thoughts to You and I commit to pray in obedience to what You reveal.

Word:

Date:

Joy

Heavenly Father, I pray that You will bless my grandchildren with the joy that comes from knowing You. You alone will be their joy and peace. Fill them completely with Your joy so that they will not pursue the world's pleasure. You alone will be their delight and peace. They will rejoice in Your Name all day long; they will exult in Your righteousness. May the joy of the Lord be their strength and stronghold. May they find their delight in the Almighty and lift their faces to You. May everlasting joy crown their heads. May gladness and joy overtake them, and sighing and sorrow flee away. May my grandchildren be blessed, for they will learn to acclaim You and walk in Your Presence. And though my grandchildren have not seen You, Lord, may they love You; even though they do not see You face to face now, may my grandchildren believe in You and be filled with an inexpressible wonder and delight. You will make known to my grandchildren the path of life; You will fill them with joy in Your Presence, with eternal pleasures at Your right hand. I pray this in the Name of Your Son Jesus. Amen.

(Phil. 4: 4; Neh. 8:10; Ps. 89:15–16; Job 22: 26;
Is. 51: 11; 1 Peter 1: 8)

Father, as I sit quietly before You praying for my grandchildren, is there any word, Scripture, insight, or particular situation related to joy which concerns my grandchildren that You want to bring to my heart? I surrender my thoughts to You and I commit to pray in obedience to what You reveal.

Word:

Date:

Justice

Heavenly Father, I pray that my grandchildren will love justice as You do, and that they will act justly in all they do. For You, Lord, are rigidly righteous, You love righteous deeds; the upright shall behold Your face; You behold the upright. You have shown my grandchildren what is good. Your Word reveals what You require of them ~ to do justly, and to love kindness and mercy, and to humble themselves and walk humbly with You. Father, may they not be moved by the crowd to wrongful action. When they give testimony, may they not pervert justice by siding with the many. May they neither show partiality to the poor nor favoritism to the great, but judge their neighbors fairly. Endow my grandchildren with Your justice, O God, with Your righteousness. May my grandchildren have Your heart towards the poor ~ for the righteous care about justice for the poor, but the wicked have no such concern. May they give justice to orphans and widows, show love to the foreigners living among us and give them food and clothing. I pray my grandchildren will love justice, and that they will act justly in all they do. In Your Son's Name. Amen.

(Ps. 11: 7; Micah 6:8; Ex 23:2; Lev 19: 15; Ps 72:1; Ps 106: 3; Prov 8: 20; Deut. 10: 18; Prov 29: 7)

Father, as I sit quietly before You praying for my grandchildren, is there any word, Scripture, insight, or particular situation related to this topic of justice which concerns my grandchildren that You want to bring to my heart? I surrender my thoughts to You and I commit to pray in obedience to what You reveal.

Word:

Date:

Leadership

Heavenly Father, Your church is in need of leaders who hold Your values, the spiritual values that advance Your Kingdom in the world. I pray that my grandchildren will become true spiritual leaders who know Your mind and Your heart. Your call to leadership always includes Your provision of the characteristics necessary to lead. By Your grace they can model Your values, but only Your Spirit can plant values deep and strong in their hearts. As my grandchildren grow, Lord God, teach them that leadership begins with servanthood. Help them to respect others, to be spiritually sensitive to Your people. Help them to enable the Body to sense the call and guidance of the Holy Spirit clearly and powerfully. Give them a healthy, strong, daily infilling of Your Spirit. Give them a deep longing for the fulfillment of Your Kingdom, for living the values that will take Your Church forward. As they ache toward this fulfillment, infuse the right values in their hearts. Make them leaders after Your own heart, guiding with knowledge and understanding, able to distinguish the significant from the trivial. Let my grandchildren become the effective leaders of the future, bringing Your Body to unity as they bring Jesus Christ to the world. I pray this in Jesus' Name. Amen.

(1 Sam. 12:2; Acts 9:15; 1 King 3: 7; Jer. 3: 15)

Father, as I sit quietly before You praying for my grandchildren, is there any word, Scripture, insight, or particular situation related to leadership which concerns my grandchildren that You want to bring to my heart? I surrender my thoughts to You and I commit to pray in obedience to what You reveal.

Word:

Date:

Mercy

Heavenly Father, when my grandchildren are offended or harmed, their first instinct may be to retaliate. I pray that they will instead yield themselves to the stirring of Your Holy Spirit, and that they will become people who extend mercy, for their Father is a God of mercy. Even though we have so often rebelled against You, You, Lord God, are merciful and forgiving. Mercy has always been Your kindness towards me and my family. Your Word says that You showed Your love to those who were called "Not My loved ones"; You said "You are My people" to those called "Not My people."

May my grandchildren be merciful, for blessed are the merciful; they will be shown mercy. Yet judgment without mercy will be shown to anyone who has not been merciful. May my grandchildren become people aware of the needs of those around them, sensitive to people who are in want and pain. Give them eyes to see the homeless, hands to feed the poor, hearts to mend wounded souls, feet to take the Gospel to the world. May they have compassion on the lost and not be ashamed of the Gospel, for the Good News of Jesus Christ is Your power bringing salvation to everyone who believes. May they be slow to judge others and quick to extend understanding. Give them hearts full of mercy. In Jesus' Name, I pray. Amen.

(Hosea 2:23; Daniel 9: 9; Matthew 5: 7; Luke 6:36; James 2:13; Romans 1: 16)

Father, as I sit quietly before You praying for my grandchildren, is there any word, Scripture, insight, or particular situation related to mercy which concerns my grandchildren that You want to bring to my heart? I surrender my thoughts to You and I commit to pray in obedience to what You reveal.

Word:

Date:

Noble Character

Heavenly Father, I pray that my grandchildren will demonstrate noble character. Nobility is not a commonly celebrated virtue in today's culture, but it represents many godly characteristics: excellence, honor, high morals, high-mindedness, and magnanimity. I pray that my grandchildren will be noble-minded and noble-hearted people, responding to Your grace with perseverance.

In a great house there are not only vessels of gold and silver, but also utensils of wood and earthenware. Some are for honorable and noble use and some for menial and ignoble use. Your Word says that if a man cleanses himself from what is ignoble and unclean, and separates himself from contact with contaminating and corrupting influences, he will then be a vessel set apart and useful for honorable and noble purposes, consecrated and profitable to the Master, fit and ready for any good work. Your Word also says that the "seed" which falls in the good soil represents the people who, hearing the Word, retain it in a noble and virtuous and worthy heart, and steadily bring forth fruit with patience. I pray that my grandchildren will prove themselves by their willingness to undertake any good work. May my grandchildren be of noble character. May they also demonstrate the nobility of their disposition by their readiness to accept and welcome the message of the Gospel of Jesus Christ, as the Bereans rather than as those at Thessalonica. They will have an inclination of mind and eagerness, searching and examining the Scriptures daily to determine the truth of what they had been taught. May my grandchildren test all things by the Scriptures, reverencing them as the judge of all truth and submitting to their authority in all matters of life and godliness. For the sake of our Lord, this I pray. Amen.

(2 Tim. 2: 20–21 TAB; Luke 8: 15 TAB; Acts 17:11)

Father, as I sit quietly before You praying for my grandchildren, is there any word, Scripture, insight, or particular situation related to my grandchildren developing noble character that You want to bring to my heart? I surrender my thoughts to You and I commit to pray in obedience to what You reveal.

Word:

Date:

Patience

Heavenly Father, I pray to You Who are so patient with me, so slow to anger. Develop in my grandchildren this fruit of the spirit ~ patience. For whatever was written in former days was written for my grandchildren's learning, that by their steadfast and patient endurance and the encouragement drawn from the Scriptures, they might hold fast to and cherish hope. Jesus is their model of infinite patience. When my grandchildren are faced with obstacles, I pray that instead of despairing, my grandchildren will exult and triumph in their troubles and rejoice in their sufferings, knowing that pressure and affliction and hardship are producing patient and unswerving endurance. This will be hard for them to accept when they are in the midst of trials. I know from Your Word that endurance develops maturity of character. And character of this sort produces the habit of joyful and confident hope. I pray that my grandchildren will be still and rest in You, Lord; I pray they will wait for You and patiently lean on You; I pray that they will not worry about those who prosper from wicked schemes. I pray they will cease from anger and turn from their rage. May they not envy others ~ it only leads to harm. May You, the God Who gives the power of patient steadfastness and Who supplies encouragement, grant my grandchildren an ability to live in harmony and sympathy towards others. I pray my grandchildren will wait patiently and expectantly for You, Lord; and You will incline Yourself to them and hear their cry. My grandchildren are surrounded by a great cloud of witnesses who have borne testimony to the Truth. Help them to strip off and throw aside every encumbrance and the sin which so readily and deftly clings to and entangles them; and let them run with patient endurance and steady and active persistence the appointed course of the race that is set before them. In Jesus' Name, I pray. Amen.

(Rom. 15: 4–5; Rom. 5: 3–4; Ps. 37: 7–8; Ps. 40: 1;
Heb. 12: 1 TAB)

Father, as I sit quietly before You praying for my grandchildren, is there any word, Scripture, insight, or particular situation related to patience which concerns my grandchildren that You want to bring to my heart? I surrender my thoughts to You and I commit to pray in obedience to what You reveal.

Word:

Date:

Peacemaker

Heavenly Father, O, that my grandchildren would be peace-makers on the earth! Deceit is in the hearts of those who devise evil, but for those who are planning peace, there is such joy. May my grandchildren be counselors of peace. Your Word says peacemakers are blessed, for they will be called sons of God. May my grandchildren make every effort to do what leads to peace and to mutual edification. Your Word asks, "Who is wise and understanding?" You answer that it is those who demonstrate wisdom by their good life and by deeds done in the humility that comes from wisdom. May my grandchildren demonstrate this godly wisdom, living lives of steady goodness so that only good deeds will pour forth. Keep them from harboring bitter envy and selfish ambition in their hearts. Keep them from boasting and from denying the truth. For such "wisdom" does not come down from heaven but is earthly, unspiritual, and motivated by the devil. Where there is envy and selfish ambition, there they will find disorder and every kind of evil practice. But the wisdom that comes from heaven is first of all pure. It is also peace-loving, considerate, submissive, and willing to yield to others. It is full of mercy and good fruit. It shows no impartiality and is always sincere. Those who are peacemakers will sow seeds of peace and reap a harvest of righteousness. May my grandchildren be sowers of peace throughout their lives. I pray this in the Name of Your Son. Amen.

(Prov. 12: 20; Matt 5: 9; Rom 14: 19; James 3: 13–18 NIV)

Father, as I sit quietly before You praying for my grandchildren, is there any word, Scripture, insight, or particular situation related to my grandchildren and their role of peacemaker that You want to bring to my heart? I surrender my thoughts to You and I commit to pray in obedience to what You reveal.

Word:

Date:

Praise

I bless and gratefully praise You, Lord. My soul and all the deepest reaches within me bless Your holy name! Father, as my grandchildren grow, I pray that they will extol You, O God, O King; I pray they will bless Your name forever and ever with grateful, affectionate praise. Make their voices be heard in praise of You. I pray that my grandchildren will thank You in everything, no matter what the circumstances may be; I pray they will be thankful and give thanks, for this is Your will for them who are in Christ Jesus, the Revealer and Mediator of that will. Through Him, therefore, may my grandchildren constantly and at all times offer up to You a sacrifice of praise, which is the fruit of their lips that thankfully acknowledge and confess and glorify Your name. May my grandchildren receive "peace, peace, which comes to him who is far off and to him who is near!" May the peace and harmony in their souls, which comes from Christ, rule continually in their hearts. You will decide and settle with finality all questions that arise in their minds, and they will remain in that peaceful state to which as members of Christ's one body, they are called to live. You promise that You create the fruit of their lips, and that You will make their lips blossom anew with speech in thankful praise. May my grandchildren bring their petitions and return to You, Lord. May they cry out to You: "Forgive all our sins and graciously receive us, so that we may offer you the sacrifice of praise." All Your works shall praise You, O Lord, and Your loving ones, my grandchildren, shall bless You. Affectionately and gratefully shall Your saints confess and praise You! In Jesus' Name, I pray. Amen.

(Ps 103: 1; Ps. 145:1; Psalm 66: 8; Col. 3: 15; 1 Thess. 5: 18; Heb. 13: 15; Is. 57: 19; Hos. 14: 2; Ps. 145: 10)

Father, as I sit quietly before You praying for my grandchildren, is there any word, Scripture, insight, or particular situation related to praise which concerns my grandchildren that You want to bring to my heart? I surrender my thoughts to You and I commit to pray in obedience to what You reveal.

Word:

Date:

Purity

Heavenly Father, I pray that my grandchildren will be pure in Your sight: for if they are pure and upright, even now You will rouse Yourself on their behalf and restore them to their rightful place. Who may ascend the hill of the LORD? Who may stand in His holy place? He who has clean hands and a pure heart, who does not lift up his soul to an idol or swear by what is false: he will receive blessing from the LORD and vindication from God his Savior. Create in my grandchildren a pure heart, O God, and renew a steadfast spirit within them. How can a young person keep his way pure? By living according to Your Word. You, LORD, detest the thoughts of the wicked, but those of the pure are pleasing to You. Even a child is known by his actions, by whether his conduct is pure and right. May my grandchildren be pure in heart, for they will be blessed and they will see You. To the pure You show yourself pure, but to the crooked You show yourself shrewd. May my grandchildren do everything without complaining or arguing, so that they may become blameless and pure, Your children without fault in a crooked and depraved generation. May they shine like stars in the universe, offering forth the word of life, so that they may rejoice on the day of Christ that they did not run or labor in vain. May my grandchildren think on those things that are true: whatever is noble, whatever is right, whatever is pure, whatever is lovely, whatever is admirable, whatever is excellent or praiseworthy. May they flee the evil desires of youth, and pursue righteousness, faith, love, and peace, along with those who call on the Lord out of a pure heart. In Jesus' Name, I pray. Amen.

(2 Sam 22: 27; Ps 24: 3–5 NIV; Ps 51:10; Ps. 119: 9; Prov. 15: 26;
Prov. 20: 11; Matt 5: 8; Phil 2: 14–16; Phil 4: 8; 2 Tim 2: 22)

Father, as I sit quietly before You praying for my grandchildren, is
there any word, Scripture, insight, or particular situation related to
purity which concerns my grandchildren that You want to bring to
my heart? I surrender my thoughts to You and I commit to pray in
obedience to what You reveal.

Word:

Date:

Restraint

Heavenly Father, as my grandchildren grow and develop their own personalities and wills, I know they will have moments of defiance. Their frustration will sometimes cause them to lash out. Selfishness will result in their demanding their own way. I ask You to uncover any anger that may abide in my grandchildren. Your Word is clear that anger does not lead to righteousness, but lodges in the bosom of fools. I petition now for Your inner working which will produce in my grandchildren a desire to rid themselves of any anger that may be a stumbling block in their walk with You. May my grandchildren be quick to listen, slow to speak, and slow to become angry: for a soft answer turns away wrath, but grievous words stir up anger. May they learn that he who is slow to anger is better than the mighty; he who rules his own spirit is better than he who takes a city. May they learn that good sense makes a man restrain his anger, and it is his glory to overlook a transgression or an offense. I pray my grandchildren will not be easily provoked. May all bitterness, indignation, and bad temper; may all resentment and quarreling; may all slander and all abusive or blasphemous language be banished from my grandchildren. May no malice, spite, ill will, or baseness of any kind reside in their hearts. May they become useful and helpful and kind to all people, tenderhearted, compassionate, understanding, and loving-hearted, forgiving readily and freely, as You, through Jesus, forgave them. When my grandchildren become angry, I pray they will not sin, nor ever let their exasperation, fury, or indignation last until the sun goes down. In Jesus' Name, I pray. Amen.

(James 1: 19–20; Prov. 19: 11; Eccl. 7: 9; Eph. 4: 31–32;
Prov. 16:32; Prov. 15: 1; Eph. 4: 26)

Father, as I sit quietly before You praying for my grandchildren, is there any word, Scripture, insight, or particular situation related to this topic of anger which concerns my grandchildren that You want to bring to my heart? I surrender my thoughts to You and I commit to pray in obedience to what You reveal.

Word:

Date:

Self - Control

Heavenly Father, I often observe that people place no control over their passions and selfish demands. I often hear, "This world is spinning out of control." Give my grandchildren, I pray, a different testimony for a watching world. May my grandchildren become people who practice self-control through the empowerment of Your Spirit, for the fruit of the Spirit is love, joy, peace, patience, kindness, goodness, faithfulness, gentleness, and self-control. Let them be different from others around them, who are asleep; let my grandchildren be alert and self-controlled. You do not give them a spirit of timidity, but You give them a spirit of power and of love and of calm and well-balanced mind. Your grace will train them to reject and renounce all ungodliness and worldly passions, so that they will live discreet, temperate, self-controlled, upright, devout, spiritually whole lives in this present world. May they add diligence to the divine promises. Enable them to employ every effort in exercising their faith to develop virtue, and in exercising virtue develop knowledge, and in exercising knowledge develop self-control, and in exercising self-control develop steadfastness, patience, and endurance. By exercising steadfastness, may they develop godliness, and in exercising godliness, develop brotherly affection, and in exercising brotherly affection, develop Christian love. In a world that will not yield its selfishness and continually demands attention, may my grandchildren demonstrate self-control. I pray this in Jesus' Name. Amen.

(Gal. 5: 22–23; 1 Thessalonians 5: 6; 2 Tim. 1: 7;Titus 2: 12;
2 Peter 1: 5–7)

Father, as I sit quietly before You praying for my grandchildren, is there any word, Scripture, insight, or particular situation related to self-control which concerns my grandchildren that You want to bring to my heart? I surrender my thoughts to You and I commit to pray in obedience to what You reveal.

Word:

Date:

Servant - Hearted

Heavenly Father, I pray that my grandchildren will worship the Lord their God, and You alone will they serve. I pray that my grandchildren will reverently fear You, will walk in Your ways, and will love and serve You with all their hearts, minds, and entire beings. Would You, Lord of Hosts, say of my grandchildren, "They shall be Mine in that day when I publicly recognize and openly declare them to be My jewels, My special possession, My unique treasure. I will spare them, as a man spares his own son who serves him." I pray that my grandchildren will seek to please You, not other people, in their thoughts and actions. May they be called servants of a God Who is alive and true and genuine.

You will enlighten their hearts so that they will be able to grasp the concept of servanthood. May they learn that they are here on earth to serve You first, then one another, with the grace and strength that You provide. They must learn that whoever wants to become great must be a servant; and whoever wants to be first, must be a slave, just as the Son of Man did not come to be served but to serve, and to give His life as a ransom for many. My grandchildren were called to be free. I pray that they will not use their freedom to indulge their sinful nature; rather, I pray that they will serve one another in love. May they know that the entire law is summed up in a single command: "Love your neighbor as yourself." May my grandchildren use whatever spiritual gift they have received to serve others, faithfully administering Your grace in its various forms. Remind them as they are growing in their faith that everything they have, everything they are, and everything they do is from You and for You. May they serve You to the glory of Your Name. Amen.

(Matt. 4: 10b; Deut. 10:12; Malachi 3: 17 TAB; Mark 10: 43–45;
Heb. 9:14; Deut. 6: 13; Matt. 20: 26–28; Gal 5: 13–14;
1 Peter 4: 10–11)

Father, as I quietly sit before You praying for my grandchildren, is there any word, Scripture, insight, or particular situation related to this topic of being servant-hearted which concerns my grandchildren that You want to bring to my heart? I surrender my thoughts to You and I commit to pray in obedience to what You reveal.

Word:

Date:

Strength

Heavenly Father, I pray that my grandchildren will always have an attitude and expectancy that they can do all things through You Who gives them Your strength to face the issues and problems of life. They will have strength for all things because it is Jesus Who empowers them. They are ready for anything and equal to anything because He infuses them with inner strength; they are self-sufficient in Christ's sufficiency. You will say to them, "My grace is enough for you. It is sufficient against any danger and enables you to bear trouble. My strength and power show themselves most effective in your weakness." Therefore, may my grandchildren all the more gladly glory in their weaknesses and infirmities, so that the strength and power of Christ the Messiah may rest (yes, may pitch a tent over and dwell) upon them! Yet amidst all difficult challenges, my grandchildren are more than conquerors and will gain a surpassing victory through Jesus Who loves them. Whatever may be their task, I pray that they will work at it with all their hearts, as something done for the Lord and not for men. They can do this in Your strength and in the Name of Your Son. Amen.

(Phil 4: 13; 2 Cor. 12: 9 TAB; Rom 8: 37; Col 3: 23)

Father, as I sit quietly before You praying for my grandchildren, is there any word, Scripture, insight, or particular situation related to strength which concerns my grandchildren that You want to bring to my heart? I surrender my thoughts to You and I commit to pray in obedience to what You reveal.

Word:

Date:

Unafraid

Holy Father, there are many things that could cause my grand-children to tremble: new or unfamiliar situations; their parents leaving them with sitters; school tests and reports; aggressive children on the playground; medical treatments; standing up for You. These are rehearsals for times when they must be courageous as adults. When my grandchildren are afraid, I pray they will learn to put their confidence in You. May my grandchildren always be courageous and strong and firm in their character and in their actions. May they learn not to fear nor be in terror, for it is the LORD Who goes with them; You will not fail nor forsake them. May they be strong and very courageous, careful to obey all Your laws; may they not turn from it to the right or to the left, so that they may be successful wherever they go. Have You not commanded them: "Be strong and courageous. Do not be terrified; do not be discouraged, for the LORD your God will be with you wherever you go." Have You not said, "Be strong and courageous. Do not be afraid or discouraged because of the vast army against you, for there is a greater power with you than with them." May my grandchildren speak the word of God courageously and fearlessly. Thank You, Holy Spirit, that You will bring these precepts to my grandchildren's remembrance when they are tempted to be afraid. They will trust in their God. In the Name of Jesus, I pray. Amen.

(Deut. 31: 6; .Joshua 1: 7,9 NIV; 2 Chron 32: 7; Phil 1: 14; Ps. 27: 1–3)

Father, as I sit quietly before You praying for my grandchildren, is there any word, Scripture, insight, or particular situation related to fear which concerns my grandchildren that You want to bring to my heart? I surrender my thoughts to You and I commit to pray in obedience to what You reveal.

Word:

Date:

Wisdom

Heavenly Father, as a grandparent, I boast, "My grandchild is so smart! Isn't he clever?" Forgive me for this short-sightedness, for in my heart I know that human intelligence comes from Your hand and is not anything this child did to receive it. The higher vision You give is to earnestly seek Your gift of wisdom for my grandchildren. I pray that they will know that the fear of the Lord is the beginning of knowledge and that only fools despise wisdom and discipline. Your Word instructs them to find out what pleases You. You tell them that they must not be foolish, but understand what Your will is. As my grandchildren grow, let them walk wisely in Your ways and be delighted with Your wisdom. Then they will commit everything they do to You and trust You to show them the blessings of obedience. Let their actions reflect the light of Your goodness, righteousness, truth, and wisdom in all they do. Day by day, fulfill all Your plans for them. May they always trust in the LORD with all their hearts and lean not on their own understanding; in all their ways may they acknowledge You, and You will make their paths straight. Will You instruct them and teach them in the way they should go? Will You counsel them and watch over them? May they please You so that You will give them wisdom, knowledge, and happiness. Surely You desire truth in the inner parts; You will teach them wisdom in the inmost place. Thank You that You will make my grandchildren wise in the things of the Lord. In Jesus' Name, I pray. Amen.

(Prov. 1:7; Ps. 37: 4–6; Eph. 5: 8–10; 15–17; Prov. 3: 5–6;
Ps. 32:8; Eccl 2: 26; Ps. 51:6; Ps. 16:11)

Father, as I sit quietly before You praying for my grandchildren, is there any word, Scripture, insight, or particular situation regarding wisdom which concerns my grandchildren that You want to bring to my heart? I surrender my thoughts to You and I commit to pray in obedience to what You reveal.

Word:

Date:

Zeal

Father, when I first opened my heart to You to receive Your Son as my Savior, I received a passion, a fervor, an intensity of love for You. Your Word reveals that it is You Who plants earnest zeal in the hearts of Your people. Jeremiah said that in his mind and heart it was as if there were a burning fire shut up in his bones. He became weary of enduring and holding it in; he could not contain his zeal for You. Isaiah said he would not keep silent, he would not remain quiet until Jerusalem shone like the dawn and her salvation like a blazing torch. Apollos, a native of Alexandria, was a cultured and eloquent man, well versed and mighty in the Scriptures. He had been instructed in the way of the Lord, and burning with spiritual zeal, he spoke and taught diligently and accurately the things concerning Jesus. He spoke fearlessly and boldly in the synagogue. Jesus' disciples identified with the words of the psalmist who said, "Zeal, the fervor of love for Your house, will eat me up. I am consumed with jealousy for the honor of Your house." Lord, I pray that my grandchildren will be zealous for the Gospel of Jesus Christ. May they be characterized by ardent, active, devoted diligence to Your Son and to the advance of His Kingdom. Like Timothy, may they abound in faith, expressing themselves in knowledge and all zeal. May they never hold back from speaking what they have seen and heard. May they never lag in zeal and in earnest endeavor; may they be aglow and burning with the Spirit, zealously serving You, all their days. In Jesus' Name, I pray.

(Rev. 3: 19; 2 Cor. 8: 16–17; Jer. 20: 9; Is. 62: 1; Acts 18: 24–26; John 2: 17; Ps. 69: 9; Acts 4: 20; Romans 12: 11)

Father, as I sit quietly before You praying for my grandchildren, is there any word, Scripture, insight, or particular situation regarding zealousness which concerns my grandchildren that You want to bring to my heart? I surrender my thoughts to You and I commit to pray in obedience to what You reveal.

Word:

Date:

Prayers for Receipt of God's Gifts

Answered Prayer

Heavenly Father, You have seen and known the outpouring cries and petitions from me, a grateful grandmother. Your Word reveals that "an angel, who has a golden censer, stands at Your altar and offers incense with the prayers of all the saints before Your throne. The smoke of the incense, together with the prayers of the saints, goes up before You from the angel's hand." I ask You to seal the work of the Holy Spirit that has begun in the lives of my grandchildren as I pour out my heart before You. I pray that You will not allow the enemy to steal or rob or pillage anything that is of You. I ask You to establish in faith and trust each prayer I have spoken that is aligned with Your will for my grandchildren. I ask that You bring peace and assurance in each request. *(Rev. 8: 3–4)*

I acknowledge that You are present in my solitary prayer time. I rejoice over any answered prayer in the lives of my grandchildren who have needed Your mercy. I ask for Your protection and covering over each grandchild as he receives healing and revelation ~ in mind, body or spirit.

Evening, and morning, and at noon, I will pray, and cry aloud: and You will hear my voice. *(Ps. 55: 17 NKJV)*

I will rise during the night and cry out. I will pour out my heart like water to You, Lord. I will lift up my hands to You in prayer. I plead for my children and my grandchildren. *(Lam. 2: 19)*

You are always ready to ask, "What do you want Me to do for you?" *(Mark 10: 51)*

You cry, "Listen to Me! You can pray for anything, and if you believe, you will have it." *(Mark 11: 24)*

If I remain in You and Your words remain in me, I may ask whatever I wish, and it will be given to me. *(John 15: 7)*

In that day I will no longer ask anything of You. This is the truth: You, my Father will give me whatever I ask in Jesus' name. I will ask and I will receive, and my joy will be complete. *(John 16: 23–24)*

But as for me, I watch in hope for the LORD, I wait for God my Savior; my God will hear me. *(Micah 7:7 NIV)*

Since ancient times no one has heard, no ear has perceived, no eye has seen any God besides You, Who acts on behalf of those who wait for Him. *(Isaiah 64: 4 NIV)*

I wait for You, LORD, my soul waits, and in Your Word I put my hope. My soul waits for the Lord more than watchmen wait for the morning, more than watchmen wait for the morning. *(Psalm 130: 5–6 NIV)*

Thank You for answered prayers. Amen.

Father, as I quietly sit before You praying for my grandchildren, help my prayers conform to Your Spirit. Give me any word, Scripture, insight, or particular situation related to this topic which concern my grandchildren that You want to bring to my heart. I surrender my thoughts to You and I commit to pray in obedience to what You reveal.

Word:

Date:

Blessed - Matthew 5:1—12

Heavenly Father, I pray that my grandchildren will be blessed. Your Word tells me that to be blessed means that they will be happy and they will be envied. To be blessed means they will be spiritually prosperous with life-joy and satisfaction in Your favor and salvation, regardless of their outward conditions. To be blessed means they will be filled with a happiness which comes from experiencing Your favor, and conditioned by the revelation of Your matchless grace.

May my grandchildren be blessed when they are poor in spirit ~ when they are humble and consider themselves insignificant and realize their need for You ~ for theirs will be the kingdom of heaven.

May my grandchildren be blessed when they mourn, for they will be comforted.

May my grandchildren be blessed by being patient and long-suffering, gentle and lowly, for the whole earth will belong to them.

May my grandchildren be blessed when they hunger and are thirsty for righteousness. They will receive in full and be completely satisfied.

May my grandchildren be blessed by being merciful, for they will be shown mercy.

May they be blessed by being pure in heart, for then they will see You, God!

May they be blessed by being the makers and maintainers of peace, for they will be called the sons of God!

May my grandchildren be blessed when they are persecuted for righteousness' sake, when they do what is right in Your sight and live for You, for theirs will be the kingdom of heaven.

May my grandchildren be blessed when people revile them and mock them and persecute them and say all kinds of evil things against them falsely because they are Your followers. For they will be glad and supremely joyful, for their reward in heaven is great. In this same way, people persecuted the prophets who were before them. I ask, Lord, that my grandchildren be spiritually blessed, through Your Holy Spirit. In Jesus' Name, I pray. Amen.

Father, as I sit quietly before You praying for my grandchildren, is there any word, Scripture, insight, or particular situation related to this topic which concerns my grandchildren that You want to bring to my heart? I surrender my thoughts to You and I commit to pray in obedience to what You reveal.

Word:

Date:

Bread

Heavenly Father, as a grandmother, I have been young and now I am older; yet I have not seen the righteous forsaken, nor my descendants begging for bread. Your bread will be given to my grandchildren; Your water will be sure. The ravens brought your prophet bread and meat in the morning, and bread and meat in the evening, and Elijah drank from the brook. You, God, will supply all my grandchildren's needs according to Your riches in Glory through Christ Jesus. May they be content with such things as they have. For Jesus Himself has said, "I will never leave you nor forsake you." On occasion, Lord, You may humble my grandchildren and allow them to go hungry, feeding them only with manna . . . that they may know that man shall not live by bread alone; but man lives by every word that proceeds from the mouth of the Lord. Jesus said, "My Father gives you the true bread from heaven. For the bread of God is He Who comes down from heaven and gives life to the world." May my grandchildren say, "Lord, give us this bread always!" I pray this in the Name of Your Son, Jesus. Amen.

(Ps. 37: 25; Is. 33: 16; 1 Kings 17: 6; Phil 4: 19; Matt 6: 11;
Deut. 8: 3; John 6: 32–34 NLT)

Father, as I sit quietly before You praying for my grandchildren, is there any word, Scripture, insight, or particular situation related to this topic of my grandchildren being desperate for You that You want to bring to my heart? I surrender my thoughts to You and I commit to pray in obedience to what You reveal.

Word:

Date:

Chosen

Father, there will be times in my grandchildren's lives when they are overlooked. It may be for an honor they had hoped for. They may not be chosen for a team. Perhaps a group of peers will exclude them. May they know that they have been selected, chosen by You for Your very own. Many are invited, but few are chosen. My grandchildren are chosen. They are a kingdom of priests, Your holy nation, Your very own possession. This is so they can show others Your goodness, for You have called them out of darkness into Your wonderful light. My grandchildren will share in the prosperity of Your chosen ones. No one can bring any charge against God's elect; no one can come forward and accuse or impeach those whom You have chosen. May my grandchildren clothe themselves, therefore, as Your own chosen ones, Your own picked representatives, who are purified and holy and well-beloved by You, putting on priestly garments. May they work hard to prove that they really are among those You have called and have chosen. Doing this, they will never stumble or fall away. May their behavior be marked by tenderhearted mercy, kind feeling, a lowly opinion of themselves, gentle ways, and patience. In Jesus, they are made Your heritage and they obtain an inheritance, for they have been chosen beforehand in accordance with Your purpose. You work out everything in agreement with the counsel and design of Your own will. You have prepared places in heaven for those You have chosen. At the End of Time, You will send forth Your angels with the sound of a mighty trumpet blast, and You will gather together Your chosen ones from the farthest ends of the earth. The Lamb will defeat the enemy because Jesus is Lord over all lords and King over all kings, and his people are the called and chosen and faithful ones. Thank You, dear Savior, for choosing my grandchildren for Your own for all of eternity. They will receive a rich welcome into Your Kingdom. Amen.

(Matt. 22: 14; Mark 13: 20; 1 Thess. 1:4; Rom. 8: 33; Eph 1: 11;
Ps. 106: 5; Mark 10: 40; Matt. 24: 31; Rev. 17: 14; 2 Peter 1: 11)

Father, as I sit quietly before You praying for my grandchildren, is there any word, Scripture, insight, or particular situation related to this topic of being chosen which concerns my grandchildren that You want to bring to my heart? I surrender my thoughts to You and I commit to pray in obedience to what You reveal.

Word:

Date:

Circumcised (Colossians 2:6–15)

Almighty God, I pray that as my grandchildren have accepted Christ Jesus as their Lord, may they walk, regulate their lives, and conduct themselves in obedience to Him. May their roots be firmly and deeply planted in Jesus, so that they may draw up nourishment from Him. May they grow in faith, strong and vigorous in the truth they are taught, abounding and overflowing in it with thanksgiving. May my grandchildren see to it that no one leads them astray with empty philosophy and high-sounding nonsense that come from human thinking and from the evil powers of this world, and not from Christ. For in Christ the fullness of the Godhead lives ~ Father, Son, and Holy Spirit ~ and my grandchildren are complete through their union with Christ. He is the Lord over every ruler and authority in the universe. When my grandchildren commit their lives to Christ, they are "circumcised," but not by a physical procedure. It is a spiritual act ~ the cutting away of their sinful nature. For they were buried with Christ when they were baptized. And with Him they are raised to a new life because they trust Your mighty power, which raised Christ from the dead. Before accepting Jesus, they were dead because of their sins and because their sinful nature was not yet cut away. But You have made my grandchildren alive with Christ. You forgive all their sins. You cancel the record that contains the charges against them. You took it and destroyed it by nailing it to the Cross of Jesus. In this way, You disarmed the evil rulers and authorities. Jesus shamed them publicly by His victory over them in His death and resurrection. This is a gift to my grandchildren too awesome to completely comprehend. I marvel that You love us so much that

You sacrificed Your Son on our behalf. I claim this gift for my life and for the lives of my grandchildren. Thank You for these promises, in Jesus' Name. Amen.

(Colossians 2: 6–15)

Father, as I sit quietly before You praying for my grandchildren, is there any word, Scripture, insight, or particular situation related to this topic which concerns my grandchildren that You want to bring to my heart? I surrender my thoughts to You and I commit to pray in obedience to what You reveal.

Word:

Date:

Consecrated

Lord God, My grandchildren are Your temple. Help them to glorify You by keeping their bodies pure because the Holy Spirit resides there. Teach them the great price You paid in the death of Jesus for their holiness. May they always know that their bodies are the very sanctuary of the Holy Spirit Who lives within them, Whom they have received as a gift. May they know that they are not their own, they were bought with a price, purchased with a preciousness and paid for by Jesus' death on a cross, and made His very own. May they make a decisive dedication of their bodies as living sacrifices, holy, devoted, consecrated, and well pleasing to You. This will be their offering of service and spiritual worship. It will be a difficult struggle without Your help, Lord, but may they not conform themselves to this world and this culture, fashioned after and adapted to its external, superficial customs. Rather, transform them by the entire renewal of their minds, so that they may prove for themselves what is Your good and acceptable and perfect will in Your sight for them. I pray this in Jesus' Name. Amen.

(1 Cor. 6: 19–21)

Father, as I sit quietly before You praying for my grandchildren, is there any word, Scripture, insight, or particular situation related to this topic which concerns my grandchildren that You want to bring to my heart? I surrender my thoughts to You and I commit to pray in obedience to what You reveal.

Word:

Date:

Devoted

Heavenly Father, there are many causes to which my grand-children can devote their lives. May their life cause be an unwavering devotion to the Living God. I pray that my grandchildren will be fully devoted to You. I know that no one can serve two masters. Either he will hate the one and love the other, or he will be devoted to the one and despise the other. A person cannot serve both You and mammon. Today, the mammon that robs my grandchildren of a true devotion may be deceitful riches, money, possessions, or whatever is trusted in. May my grandchildren devote themselves to the apostles' teaching and to the fellowship, to the breaking of bread, and to prayer. May they be devoted to others in the Body of Christ in brotherly love. For if they devote their hearts to You and stretch out their hands to You, if they put away the sin that is in their hand and allow no evil to dwell in their tent, then they will lift up their faces without shame; they will stand firm and without fear. Guard the hearts of my grandchildren, Lord God. Make them devoted to You. For You are their God. Save Your servants who trust in You. Father, convict my grandchildren of the devotion that You require of all who call upon Your Name. Guard them and enable them to stand firm as they trust in You and devote themselves to You. In Jesus' Name, I pray. Amen.

(Matt 6: 24; Acts 2: 42; Job 11: 13–15; Ps. 86: 2)

Father, as I sit quietly before You praying for my grandchildren, is there any word, Scripture, insight, or particular situation related to this topic which concerns my grandchildren that You want to bring to my heart? I surrender my thoughts to You and I commit to pray in obedience to what You reveal.

Word:

Date:

A Discerning Heart

Heavenly Father, my prayer for my grandchildren is that You will create within them a wise and discerning heart so that they will always be able to distinguish between right and wrong. May they be filled with the fruit of righteousness that comes from knowing and trusting in Jesus. May this be to Your glory and praise. Help my grandchildren trust in You with all their heart and lean not on their own understanding. If they will acknowledge You in all their ways, You will make their paths straight. I know that through Your precepts my grandchildren will gain wisdom. My prayer, therefore, is that they will hate every false way and that Your Word will be as a lamp to their feet and a light to their path. I pray for them as they steadily grow and increase in and by Your knowledge, beseeching You to fill them with the full, deep, and clear knowledge of Your will, giving them spiritual wisdom and understanding and discernment of spiritual things. With this infilling, may they live in a manner worthy of You, Lord, desiring to please You in all things. Jesus has been made wisdom to these children; therefore, I pray they will listen to His Voice and He will add to their learning. In Jesus' Name, I pray. Amen.

(1 Kings 3:9; Prov. 3: 1–5; Ps. 119: 104,105; Gen. 41: 39–41;
Joshua 1: 5; Col. 1: 9,10; 1 Cor. 1: 30; Eph. 5: 17)

Father, as I sit quietly before You praying for my grandchildren, is there any word, Scripture, insight, or particular situation related to discernment which concerns my grandchildren that You want to bring to my heart? I surrender my thoughts to You and I commit to pray in obedience to what You reveal.

Word:

Date:

Divine Mysteries

Father, You have said, "It is the glory of God to conceal a matter; to search out a matter is the glory of kings." You also tell us, "the secret things belong to You, but the things that are revealed belong to me and my children forever, that I may do all of the words of Your law." How amazing that You did not reveal this mystery in generations past, but chose this age to disclose Your divine plan. Your Word promises that the divine mysteries will belong to my children and my grandchildren! In accordance with Your Word, I pray that my grandchildren's hearts may be braced, comforted, cheered, and encouraged as they are knit together by strong ties of love. May they have full confidence because You have given them complete understanding of Your secret plan, which is Christ Himself. In Him lie hidden all the treasures of wisdom and knowledge. This mystery of Christ is given only by revelation. They cannot grasp it on their own. May my grandchildren come to know Jesus, for in Him is the whole fullness of Deity, the Godhead, Who continues to dwell in bodily form and gives the complete expression of the divine nature. I claim that as my grandchildren accept Jesus as their Savior, they will be in Him and will reach full spiritual stature. He is the Lord over every ruler and authority in the universe. You have made this mystery known to me and will make it known to my grandchildren. I claim this promise for my grandchildren, in the Name of Christ the Messiah, the Anointed One. Amen.

(Prov. 25: 2 NIV; Deut. 29:29; Col. 2: 2–3; Eph. 3: 3–6;
Col. 2: 9–10)

Father, as I sit quietly before You praying for my grandchildren, is there any word, Scripture, insight, or particular situation related to this topic which concerns my grandchildren that You want to bring to my heart? I surrender my thoughts to You and I commit to pray in obedience to what You reveal.

Word:

Date:

Established

Father, I am grateful that You will establish my grandchildren in Jesus. In all my longings and prayers for my grandchildren to attain a deep and abiding faith, I can hold fast to Your Word which guarantees that You, the LORD, will work out Your plans for their lives. You have made them, and Your faithful love endures forever. When my grandchildren's spiritual lives become variable ~ some days of deep earnestness, then something marring their peace to bring doubt and disappointment to their souls ~ thank You that You will confirm and make them steadfast and establish them in Christ. They can cease from trying to establish or reestablish a connection with You. You will consecrate and anoint them, enduing them with the gifts of the Holy Spirit. They can rest in Your promise that You will surely do this, for You always do just what You say, and You are the One who invited my grandchildren into this wonderful friendship with Your Son. It is a work that You delight to do, in spite of weakness and faithlessness. Jesus will make their hearts strong, blameless, and holy when they stand before You on that day when He comes for all those who belong to Him. You are faithful and will strengthen my grandchildren and set them on a firm foundation and guard them from the evil one. You, the God of all grace, will complete and make these children what they ought to be, established and grounded securely, strengthened, and settled. What peace and rest to know that You, God, watch over every hindrance, every danger, You supply every need. You will impart the ability to stand firm for Christ. You have commissioned my grandchildren, and You have identified them as Your own by placing the Holy Spirit in their hearts as the first installment of everything You will give them. May my grandchildren come to see and accept what You bring. I pray they will bear witness to the wonderful changes that come to their spiritual walks daily. May they realize they are taught by the Teacher Who plans the whole course of study uniquely tailored for each of them. May they come daily for Your lessons and follow Your guidance. May they begin each morning with the joyous surrender of all their needs and cares into their Father's hands. What a joy it is to know that You have charge and You will do it. May their faith grow stronger each new morning as they become established in Christ Jesus. Amen.

(Ps. 138: 8; 1 Cor. 1: 9; Deut. 28: 9; 1 Thess. 3: 13; 1 Peter 5: 10; 2 Cor. 1: 21–22)

Father, as I sit quietly before You praying for my grandchildren, is there any word, Scripture, insight, or particular situation related my grandchildren being established that You want to bring to my heart? I surrender my thoughts to You and I commit to pray in obedience to what You reveal.

Word:

Date:

Filled with the Holy Spirit

Heavenly Father, I receive abundant blessings this day, because I am a grandmother praying, filled with Your Holy Spirit. It is impossible to overestimate the power of this sacred filling of my soul. I know that life, comfort, light, purity, spiritual enlightenment, peace, and many other precious gifts are inseparable from the Spirit's presence in my heart.

Today I ask that You anoint my grandchildren's heads with the oil of Your Spirit, setting them apart to the holy priesthood of saints. Give them grace to minister to Your beloved people according to Your direction. As the only true purifying water, cleanse them from the taint of sin and sanctify them to holiness, working in them to will and to do Your good pleasure. As Light, may Your Holy Spirit teach them their lost estate, and reveal the Lord Jesus to them and in them, and guide them in the way of righteousness. Be the Light and Guide for my grandchildren.

As fire, Your Holy Spirit will purge them from dross, and set their consecrated nature ablaze. You are the sacrificial flame, the consuming fire, by which my grandchildren will be enabled to offer themselves as living sacrifices. As the Comforter, please dispel the cares and doubts which may mar the peace of these little servants as they grow in their knowledge of You.

Descend upon these chosen vessels as You fell upon Jesus in the River Jordan. Bear witness to their sonship as they cry "Abba, Father." As Wind, bring the breath of life to the people they will meet in their lives and minister to according to their unique calls. May they feel the power of Your Presence as they travel forth in their walk with You ~ this day and every day. I pray this in the Name of Your Son. Amen.

(Acts 2: 4; Lev. 21: 10; 1 Peter 2: 5; Rom. 12: 1; Eph. 1: 9;
Isaiah 1: 25; Matt. 3: 16; Gal. 4: 6)

Father, as I sit quietly before You praying for my grandchildren, is there any word, Scripture, insight, or particular situation related to my grandchildren being filled with the Holy Spirit that You want to bring to my heart? I surrender my thoughts to You and I commit to pray in obedience to what You reveal.

Word:

Date:

Freedom

Heavenly Father, I pray that my grandchildren will be free from any bondage that keeps them from knowing You fully and freely. May they be free from worry; from shame; free from feelings of abandonment; free from fear; free from powerlessness; free from invalidation; free from hopelessness; free from worthlessness; free from confusion; free from feeling tainted by their past actions. These bondages were nailed to the Cross. I pray that my grandchildren will know the Truth, and the Truth will set them free. I pray that if You, Jesus, make my grandchildren free, they will be free indeed. I know that there is no condemnation for my grandchildren who are in Christ Jesus, because through Christ Jesus, the law of the Spirit of life sets them free from the law of sin and death. O LORD, truly they are your servants; You have freed them from chains. You say to the captives, 'Come out,' and to those in darkness, 'Be free!' And though all have sinned and fall short of the glory of God, my grandchildren are justified freely by Your grace through the redemption that came by Christ Jesus. They have been set free from sin and have become slaves to righteousness. They have been set free from sin and have become slaves to God. The benefit they reap leads to holiness, and the result is eternal life. My grandchildren have not received the spirit of the world but the Spirit Who is from God, that they may understand what You have freely given them. You, Lord, are Spirit, and where the Spirit of the Lord is, there is freedom. Thank You for freeing these children and filling them with joy and hope. In Jesus' Name, I pray. Amen.

(John 8: 32; John 8: 36; Romans 8: 1–2; Ps. 116: 16;
Romans 3: 23–24; Romans 6: 18, 22; 1 Cor 2: 12; 2 Cor. 3: 17)

Father, as I sit quietly before You praying for my grandchildren, is there any word, Scripture, insight, or particular situation related to this topic of freedom which concerns my grandchildren that You want to bring to my heart? I surrender my thoughts to You and I commit to pray in obedience to what You reveal.

Word:

Date:

Fruit of the Holy Spirit

Lord, develop in my grandchildren the fruit of Your Spirit: love, joy, peace, patience, kindness, goodness, faithfulness, gentleness, and self-control. Because my grandchildren belong to You, let them live by Your Spirit, not by their sinful nature, and keep them in step with You. Keep them humble and thankful, ever aware that all good things come from You and all they accomplish is by Your power. You, Lord God, are the Vine and my grandchildren are the branches. If they remain in You and You in them, they will bear much fruit; apart from You, they can do nothing. If they remain in You and Your Words remain in them, they can ask anything they wish, and it will be given to them. May my grandchildren be the good soil–for what was sown on good soil represents the person who hears the Word and understands it. He produces a crop, yielding a hundred, sixty, or thirty times what was sown. May my grandchildren have Your wisdom that comes down from heaven: it is first of all pure, then peace loving, considerate, submissive, full of mercy and good fruit, impartial, and sincere. This is to Your glory: that my grandchildren bear much fruit, showing themselves to be Your disciples. You are faithful in calling them to Yourself and You are utterly trustworthy. You will do this ~ fulfilling Your call on their lives by hallowing and keeping them. In Jesus' Name, I pray. Amen.

(Gal. 5: 22–26; Phil. 4:13; John 15: 5; John 15: 7–8;
Matt. 13: 23; James 3: 17; John 15: 8)

Father, as I sit quietly before You praying for my grandchildren, is there any word, Scripture, insight, or particular situation related to the fruit of the Spirit which concerns my grandchildren that You want to bring to my heart? I surrender my thoughts to You and I commit to pray in obedience to what You reveal.

Word:

Date:

Gifts of the Holy Spirit - 1

Heavenly Father, Your Word reveals that every believer is given a significant ability by the Holy Spirit, Who equips and moves each child of God to serve in special ways to build Your Kingdom. You use the analogy of a body with many parts ~ all contributing to the function of that body, but no part being more valuable than the next. Your Word reveals that You have placed and arranged the limbs and organs in the body, each particular one of them, just as You wish and see fit and with the best adaptation. You have put each part just where You want it. Your spiritual gifts allow Your people to work rhythmically and easily with each other, efficiently and gracefully in response to Your Son, fully alive like Christ. The world watches while Your people work together in love. Concerning spiritual gifts, You do not want us ignorant.

My grandchildren will be given unique gifts to glorify You. They will work to build up Your church, the Body of Christ, until we come to such unity in our faith and knowledge of Your Son that we will be mature and full grown in the Lord. To some of my grand-children, You will give the gift of discipleship, prophecy, evangelism, and/or teaching. To others, You will give gifts of administration, discernment, encouragement, faith, giving, service, knowledge, leadership, unknown languages, interpretation of these languages, wisdom, artistic ability, intercession, celibacy, or poverty. Your Word assures me that the gifts they possess will differ as they are allotted to them by Your grace and for Your purposes. My grandchildren are yet young and I see glimpses of natural talents and intelligence and personality ~ all from Your Hand. I am eager to learn what spiritual gifts are yet to come. May my grandchildren yield themselves to be used by You. Each one, as a good steward of Your gifts, must use them for the good of others. May they fan into flame the gifts You have given. Will You verify their testimonies by signs and wonders and various miracles and by giving gifts of the Holy Spirit whenever You choose.

You promise that You give good things to those who ask. I pray my grandchildren will seek insight to unlock the possibilities of their future ministry to You through these spiritual gifts. If they lack wisdom, they will ask it of You, for You give wisdom to all men generously. You will gladly tell and will not resent their asking. Help them seek You in identifying and using the gifts You impart to them. In Jesus' Name, I pray. Amen.

(1 Cor. 12: 1, 7, 18: Eph. 4: 7, 11–13, Matt. 7: 11; Romans, 12: 6;
1 Peter 4: 10; 2 Tim. 1: 6; Heb. 2: 4; James 1: 5)

Father, as I sit quietly before You praying for my grandchildren, is there any word, Scripture, insight, or particular situation related to this topic on spiritual gifts which concerns my grandchildren that You want to bring to my heart? I surrender my thoughts to You and I commit to pray in obedience to what You reveal.

Word:

Date:

Gifts of the Holy Spirit - 2

"A generous man will prosper; he who waters shall be watered also himself." - Proverbs 11:25 NIV

Father, what an amazing promise. You teach us the great lesson: that to receive, we must give; that to accumulate, we must scatter; that to make ourselves happy, we must make others happy; and that in order to become spiritually vigorous, we must seek the spiritual growth of others. In watering others, we ourselves are watered. As my grandchildren grow to adulthood, they will begin to notice that they are uniquely fashioned to bless others. They will begin to see the ways they easily bring a word, a talent, or ability to bear on situations. Latent talents and dormant gifts will come forth into the light. Surprise them, Father! May the spiritual strength that is hidden even from my grandchildren's awareness venture forth by exercise. Help the tender compassion and sympathies they possess be activated to dry the tears of the broken-hearted, soothe the orphan's grief, and meet the needs of the poor and neglected.

My grandchildren will discover that in attempting to teach others, they gain instruction for themselves. When they offer their hands for good works, their act of service will change their hearts. When they open their mouths to sing for others, they will enter into secret places of worship with You alone. Oh, what gracious lessons some of us have learned when ministering to the sick and lost! We have gone to teach the Scriptures, but have come away embarrassed that we know so little of them. In our ministries, we have been taught Your way more perfectly for ourselves and get a deeper insight into divine truth. As my grandchildren learn to exercise their unique spiritual gifts given by the Holy Spirit, help them know that they will receive more in return as they edify the whole Body of Christ. May they be sacrificial in their use of these gifts. In Jesus' Name, I pray. Amen.

(Prov. 11: 25 NIV; Eph. 4: 12, 16)

Father, as I sit quietly before You praying for my grandchildren, is there any word, Scripture, insight, or particular situation related to this topic on using spiritual gifts which concerns my grandchildren that You want to bring to my heart? I surrender my thoughts to You and I commit to pray in obedience to what You reveal.

Word:

Date:

Grace

Heavenly Father, You are a God of grace. Your Son is full of grace and truth. You have extended Your grace, Your favor, Your loving-kindness upon me and my grandchildren. Your Word says that we are a holy people who belong to the LORD. Of all the people on earth, we have been chosen to be Your own special treasure by Your grace. You did not choose us and lavish Your love on us because we are larger or greater. It is simply because You love us. Just as our forefathers, we were rescued from our slavery with amazing power. Sin is no longer our master, for we are no longer subject to the law, which enslaves us to sin. Instead, we are free by Your grace. We understand, therefore, that You, LORD are indeed God. You are faithful and keep Your covenant for a thousand generations and constantly love those who love You and obey Your commands. I pray that my grandchildren may grow in the grace and knowledge of their Lord and Savior. May the grace of their Lord be poured out on them abundantly, along with the faith and love that are in Christ Jesus. For out of Your abundance, my grandchildren have received one grace after another and spiritual blessing upon spiritual blessing and even favor upon favor and gift heaped upon gift. May they be as Stephen who was full of grace. He was filled with Your power and worked great wonders and miracles among the people. Grace and divine blessing and peace be to my grandchildren from God the Father and from the Lord Jesus. May the grace of our Lord Jesus Christ, the love of God, and the fellowship of the Holy Spirit be with each of my grandchildren forevermore. Amen.

(John 1: 14, 16; Deut. 7: 6–9; Romans 6: 14; 2 Peter 3: 18;
1 Tim. 1: 14; Acts 6: 8; Romans 1: 7; 2 Cor. 13:14)

Father, as I sit quietly before You praying for my grandchildren, is
there any word, Scripture, insight, or particular situation related to
grace which concerns my grandchildren that You want to bring to
my heart? I surrender my thoughts to You and I commit to pray in
obedience to what You reveal.

Word:

Date:

Inheritance

Lord God, I sometimes carefully tuck away items knowing that in time my grandchildren will inherit them from me. These are earthly treasures. They in no measure match the magnitude of the heavenly inheritance that awaits them. Give my grandchildren a vision of that inheritance as even now I pray Your words over them. I pray that whatever may be my grandchildren's tasks, they will work at them heartily as something done for the Lord and not to men, knowing that from You they will receive the reward of their inheritance, for they serve the Lord Jesus Christ. They can trust that You give very great and precious promises. Through these promises as they yield their lives to You, they will be able to participate in Your divine nature and escape the world's corruption caused by evil desires. I commit my grandchildren to You. I deposit them into Your care, entrusting them to Your protection. And I commend them to the Word of Your grace, Your unmerited favor. Your Word is able to build up my grandchildren and give them their rightful inheritance among all of Your chosen and set-apart ones. The Holy Spirit Himself testifies with their spirit that my grandchildren are Your children. Because they are Your children, then they are heirs ~ heirs of God and co-heirs with Christ. They will share in Christ's sufferings in order that they may also share in His glory. May my grandchildren persevere under trial, because when they have stood the test, they will receive the crown of life that You have promised to those who love Jesus. When the Chief Shepherd appears, my grandchildren will receive the crown of glory that will never fade away. They will receive a rich and abundant entry into the eternal kingdom of our Lord and Savior Jesus Christ. In Jesus' Name. Amen.

(Col. 3: 23–24; 2 Peter 1: 4; Acts 20: 32; Rom. 8: 16–17,
James 1: 12;1 Peter 5: 4 ; 2 Peter 1: 11)

Father, as I sit quietly before You praying for my grandchildren, is there any word, Scripture, insight, or particular situation related to this topic which concerns my grandchildren that You want to bring to my heart? I surrender my thoughts to You and I commit to pray in obedience to what You reveal.

Word:

Date:

Instructed

Lord God, Your Word says that the LORD Almighty is a wonderful, all powerful Teacher. Who is a teacher like You? A wise teacher's words spur students to action and emphasize important truths. The collected sayings of the wise teacher are like guidance from a shepherd. Be my grandchildren's Teacher this day. Father, some of my grandchildren will be going to elementary or middle school. Some with be going to nursery school or mothers-day-out. Others will be safe at home, playing with their toys at their mother's feet. Some are learning to sit up. Regardless of where they are, would You be their teacher this day. Impart spiritual truth in their inner being. Perhaps it is to be obedient to those placed in authority over them. Perhaps it is how to extend mercy to a hurting friend. Even my babies and toddlers may learn the truth that You have given them loving parents to watch over them and lead them in the ways everlasting. They are safe. They can trust. Whatever You want my grandchildren to know this day, I stand beside You as a grandmother who intercedes on their behalf. Be their Teacher today and always, for Your Son teaches as One who has real authority ~ quite unlike the teachers of religious law. I pray my grandchildren will learn that a student is not greater than the Teacher. A servant is not greater than the master. May they never look back and say, "Oh, why didn't I listen to my teachers? Why didn't I pay attention to those who gave me instruction?" Let their hearts be pliable to You. Give them grace to recognize Wisdom, for the fear of the LORD is the beginning of knowledge. Only the foolish despise wisdom and discipline. Even as babies, let them know Your Presence as You gently instruct them to follow You always. I pray this in the Name of Your Son. Amen.

(Job 36: 22; Prov. 5: 13; Eccl. 12: 11; Is. 28: 29a; Matt. 7: 29; Matt 10: 24)

Father, as I sit quietly before You praying for my grandchildren, is there any word, Scripture, insight, or particular situation related to this topic which concerns my grandchildren that You want to bring to my heart? I surrender my thoughts to You and I commit to pray in obedience to what You reveal.

Word:

Date:

Known Completely

Lord, as my grandchildren grow and learn to spend quiet time with You, let them know how limitless Your love for them is. As they sit before You, by Your grace, help them understand the depth of Your sacrifice for them. Speak to their hearts Your concern for every detail of their lives. You have made them unique and precious. Let Your Spirit teach them what it means to live as children of the King of Kings. May my grandchildren have power, together with all the saints, to grasp how wide and long and high and deep is Jesus' love for them. Then they will be filled with the fullness of God when they know this love that surpasses knowledge. O LORD, you have searched my grandchildren thoroughly and have known them, even those as yet unborn. You know when they sit down to rest and when they awaken for the day. You understand their thoughts when they wander off. You sift and search out their paths and You are acquainted with all their ways. For there is not a word on their tongue still unspoken, but, behold, O Lord, You already know it. You have and will beset them to shake their complacency. You shut them in ~ behind and before, and You have laid Your hand upon them. And You, my God, will liberally supply (fill to the full) their every need according to Your riches in glory in Christ Jesus. Thank You for knowing my grandchildren and loving them completely. Amen.

(Eph. 3:18–19; Phil 4:19; Ps. 139: 1–6)

Father, as I sit quietly before You praying for my grandchildren, is there any word, Scripture, insight, or particular situation related to this topic which concerns my grandchildren that You want to bring to my heart? I surrender my thoughts to You and I commit to pray in obedience to what You reveal.

Word:

Date:

Light

Heavenly Father, You are Light and in You there is no darkness at all. As long as my grandchildren are in the world, You call them to be the light of the world. If they say they have fellowship with You, and yet go on living in spiritual darkness, they lie and are not living in the truth. For what do righteousness and wickedness have in common? Or what fellowship can light have with darkness? Jesus said, "I am the Light of the world. Whoever follows Me will never walk in darkness, but will have the light of life." If my grandchildren walk in the light as Jesus is in the light, they will have fellowship with You and with Your Son and with the Holy Spirit. The blood Jesus shed on a cross cleanses my grandchildren from all sin. If they accept this truth, then You, Father, will qualify them to be partakers of the inheritance of the saints in the light. You have delivered them from the power of darkness and have conveyed them into the kingdom of the Son of Your love. In Jesus, my grandchildren have redemption through His blood, and the forgiveness of their sins. I pray my grandchildren will be sons and daughters of light and sons and daughters of the day. They are neither of the night nor of darkness. They are the city that is set on a hill which cannot be hidden. Let the light of my grandchildren so shine before men, that the world may see their good works and glorify You, Father, Who are in heaven. Amen.

(1 John 1: 7; Matt. 5: 14; 1 John 2: 9; 1 John 1: 6; 2 Cor. 6: 14; Eph. 5: 8; John 8: 12 NIV)

Father, as I sit quietly before You praying for my grandchildren, is there any word, Scripture, insight, or particular situation related to light which concerns my grandchildren that You want to bring to my heart? I surrender my thoughts to You and I commit to pray in obedience to what You reveal.

Word:

Date:

Love - 1

Heavenly Father, I pray that my grandchildren will know the limitless love of Your Father's heart. Let them know by experience how extravagantly and unconditionally You love them. Father them with Your holy love, so they never doubt that You are working in their lives. May they see how great a love You, the Father, have bestowed on them, that they should be called and known as the children of God. I pray that You will dwell in my grandchildren's hearts through faith and that they, being rooted and grounded in love, may be able to comprehend what is the width and length and depth and height of Your love. May they know Your love which passes understanding in order that they may be filled with all the fullness of Your Spirit. I pray that my grandchildren will know that You, God, have loved each of them with an everlasting love, and with loving-kindness, You have drawn them to Yourself. I pray that my grandchildren will realize that You rejoice over them with gladness. That You quiet them with Your love and that You rejoice over them with singing. Your banner over them is love. I pray this in the Name of Your Son. Amen.

(1 John 3: 1; Eph. 3: 17–19; Jer. 31:3; Zeph. 3: 17)

Father, as I sit quietly before You praying for my grandchildren, is there any word, Scripture, insight, or particular situation related to love which concerns my grandchildren that You want to bring to my heart? I surrender my thoughts to You and I commit to pray in obedience to what You reveal.

Word:

Date:

Love - 2

Heavenly Father, in accordance with Your Word, I pray that my grandchildren will grow to know that this is love: not that they loved God, but that You loved them and sent Your Son as an atoning sacrifice for their sins. My grandchildren will love You, God, because You first loved them. Because of their faith, Christ will actually dwell (settle down, abide, and make His permanent home) in my grandchildren's hearts! May these children be rooted deep in love and founded securely on love, that they may have the power and strength to apprehend and grasp with all the saints, the experience of that love. May my grandchildren deeply come to know the love of Christ, which far surpasses mere head knowledge without experience. They will have the richest measure of Your divine Presence, and become wholly filled and flooded with Your Holy Spirit. You, God, show and clearly prove Your own love for my grandchildren by the fact that while they were still sinners, Christ died for them. May they be persuaded beyond doubt that neither death, nor life, nor angels, nor principalities, nor things impending and threatening, nor things to come, nor powers, nor height, nor depth, nor anything else in all creation will be able to separate my grandchildren from Your love which is in Christ Jesus our Lord. Amen.

(1 John 4: 10, 19; Eph. 3: 17–19; Rom. 5: 8; Rom. 8: 38–39)

Father, as I sit quietly before You praying for my grandchildren, is there any word, Scripture, insight, or particular situation related to this topic which concerns my grandchildren that You want to bring to my heart? I surrender my thoughts to You and I commit to pray in obedience to what You reveal.

Word:

Date:

Peace

Jesus, You said, "Do not let your hearts be troubled. Trust in God, trust also in Me. Peace I leave with you; My peace I give to you. I do not give to you as the world gives. Do not let your hearts be troubled and do not be afraid." Father, I pray that my grandchildren will know Your peace all their days. Let my grandchildren know the plans You have for them, plans to prosper and not to harm. Plans to give them hope and a future. In these troubled times, may You keep my grandchildren in perfect peace, their minds stayed on You, because they trust in You. I pray that my grandchildren will lie down at naptime and at night in peace and rest, for You alone, O Lord, make them dwell in safety. I pray that Jesus Himself is my grandchildren's peace. I pray that the peace of God will rule in their hearts. I pray that my grandchildren will not be anxious, but in all they face, by prayer and supplications with thanksgiving, they will tell You their concerns. May Your peace which surpasses all understanding guard their hearts and minds through Christ Jesus. Amen.

(John 14:27 NIV; Jer. 29:11; Is. 26:3; Eph. 2: 14; Ps. 4:8;
Col. 3: 15; Phil. 4: 6–7)

*Father, as I sit quietly before You praying for my grandchildren, is
there any word, Scripture, insight, or particular situation related to
peace which concerns my grandchildren that You want to bring to
my heart? I surrender my thoughts to You and I commit to pray in
obedience to what You reveal.*

Word:

Date:

Power

Lord God, my grandchildren are in need of Your power which comes from the Holy Spirit. I pray that in all things my grandchildren are more than conquerors and gain an overwhelming victory through Jesus Who loves them. My grandchildren can do all things through Christ Who strengthens them. May my grandchildren find contentment and not succumb to fear when faced with infirmities, insults, hardships, persecutions, perplexities, and distresses. When they are weak in human strength, then they are truly strong, able, and powerful in divine strength. I know, Lord God, that You are able to make all grace and earthly blessing come to my grandchildren in abundance, so that they may grab hold of Your sufficiency under all circumstances and for every need that arises. They will possess enough through Your Spirit to require no aid or support. You will abundantly equip them for every good work. I pray that Your grace will be made sufficient for my grandchildren, for Your strength is made perfect in weakness. May my grandchildren know and understand what is the immeasurable and unlimited and surpassing greatness of Your power in and for those who believe. This is demonstrated in the working of Your mighty strength. This is the same mighty power that raised Jesus from the dead and seated Him in the place of honor at Your right hand in the heavenly realms! By the action of Your power that is at work within them, You are able to carry out Your purpose in their lives. You will do superabundantly, far above all that I dare ask or think, infinitely beyond my highest prayers, thoughts, hopes, or dreams for my grandchildren. Thank You. I pray in Jesus' Name. Amen.

(Rom. 8:37; Phil 4: 1; John 14:13; 2 Cor. 9:8; 2 Cor. 12:9, 10; Eph. 1: 19–20; Eph. 3: 20)

Father, as I sit quietly before You praying for my grandchildren, is there any word, Scripture, insight, or particular situation related to appropriating Your power which concerns my grandchildren that You want to bring to my heart? I surrender my thoughts to You and I commit to pray in obedience to what You reveal.

Word:

Date:

Predestined

Heavenly Father, I pray that my grandchildren will know how precious they are to You. In Your love, You chose my grandchildren. You actually picked them out for Yourself as Your own in Christ before the foundation of the world. You established that they would be holy, consecrated, and set apart for You, blameless in Your sight. They are even above reproach, before You in love. Teach them to base their identity and security on Christ. Give them Christ-centered confidence and worth. Give them Your mind about how You see them and how You feel about them. As Your creation, help my grandchildren fully know who they are, what they have in Christ, and what they can do through Him. In Jesus they have redemption through His blood, and forgiveness of their offenses and shortcomings. This is in accordance with the riches and the generosity of Your gracious favor. Furthermore, because of Jesus, my grandchildren have received an inheritance, for You chose them from the beginning, and all things happen just as You decided long ago. Your purpose was that those early believers, who were the first to trust You, should praise You. And now my grandchildren also have heard the truth, the Good News that God saves. And when they believe in Christ, You will identify them as Your own by giving them the Holy Spirit, Whom You promised long ago. Your Holy Spirit is the guarantee that You will give my grandchildren everything You promise, and that Jesus has purchased these children to be His own people. This is one more amazing reason for me to praise my glorious God. May my grandchildren believe these astonishing truths as they grow to know You. In Jesus Name, I pray. Amen.

(Eph. 1: 4, 7, 11–14)

Father, as I sit quietly before You praying for my grandchildren, is there any word, Scripture, insight, or particular situation related to this topic of being predestined which concerns my grandchildren that You want to bring to my heart? I surrender my thoughts to You and I commit to pray in obedience to what You reveal.

Word:

Date:

Psalm 139

Father, I continue to pray that my grandchildren will grow to know how limitless Your love for them is. May they learn that Your infinite knowledge is too wonderful; it is high above them; they cannot reach it. They cannot go from Your Spirit. They cannot flee from Your presence. If they ascend up into heaven, You are there; if they make their bed in Sheol (the place of the dead), behold, You are there. If they take the wings of the morning or dwell in the uttermost parts of the sea, even there Your hand will lead them, and Your right hand will hold them. If they say, 'Surely the darkness will cover me and the night will be the only light about me,' even the darkness hides nothing from You, but the night shines as the day; the darkness and the light are both alike to You. You formed the inward parts of my grandchildren; You knit them together in their mothers' wombs. May they confess and praise You, for You are fearful and wonderful; may they praise You for the wonder of their birth! Wonderful are Your works; may their inner self know this well. Their frames were not hidden from You when they were being formed in secret and intricately and curiously wrought in mystery. Your eyes saw their unformed substance, and in Your book all the days of their lives were written before ever they took shape, when as yet there was none of them. How precious and weighty are Your thoughts toward my grandchildren, O God! How vast is the sum of them! If I could count Your thoughts about them, they would be more in number than the sand. May my grandchildren grow to know Your incredible love for each of them, I pray this in Jesus' Name. Amen.

Father, as I sit quietly before You praying for my grandchildren, is there any word, Scripture, insight, or particular situation related to this topic which concerns my grandchildren that You want to bring to my heart? I surrender my thoughts to You and I commit to pray in obedience to what You reveal.

Word:

Date:

Revealer of Secrets

"The Lord confides in those who fear Him; He makes His covenant known to them." Psalm 25:14 NIV

"Henceforth I no longer call you servants, because a servant does not know what his Master does; instead I have called you friends, for I have revealed to you everything that I have learned from My Father." John 15:15

"If it were not so, I would have told you." John 14:2 NIV

"Call to Me and I will answer you and tell you great and unsearchable things you do not know." Jer. 33: 3 NIV

Father, how grateful I am that You are the Divine Revealer of Secrets and expose my grandchildren to Your Mind and Heart. You keep back nothing which is profitable to them. I thank You that You are instructing my grandchildren in the way they should go and that You are guiding them with Your eye. I thank You for Your leading and guidance concerning Your will, Your plan, and Your purpose for their individual lives. I pray that they will hear the Voice of the Good Shepherd and that they will know You and follow You. You lead them in the paths of righteousness. Their paths are growing brighter and brighter until they reach the full light of day. Jesus is being made wisdom to my grandchildren. Confusion will not be a part of their lives. I pray that they will trust You and not lean on their own understanding. As they acknowledge You in all their ways, You are directing their paths and will show them the path of life. Thank You for the intimacy they will have with You, their King, their Lord, and their Sustainer. In Jesus' Name. Amen.

(John 10:3; Ps. 23:3; Prov. 4: 18; 1 Cor. 1: 30; Prov. 3: 5; Ps. 16: 11)

Father, as I sit quietly before You praying for my grandchildren, is there any word, Scripture, insight, or particular situation related to this topic which concerns my grandchildren that You want to bring to my heart? I surrender my thoughts to You and I commit to pray in obedience to what You reveal.

Word:

Date:

Salvation

Lord, let salvation spring up within my grandchildren whom You have chosen to serve You. May they be willing to endure anything if it will bring salvation and eternal glory in Christ Jesus. As they grow, I believe that they will come to understand what You meant when You said, "If anyone acknowledges Me publicly here on earth, I will openly acknowledge that person before My Father in heaven." I believe that You, God, have saved my grandchildren and have called them to a holy life ~ not because of anything they have done or will do, but because of Your own purpose and grace. This grace was given to them. They had nothing to do with this extraordinary gift. It was all Your doing, a gift prepared for them in Jesus long before they were given life. I pray that this will be my grandchildren's testimony to their friends, their family, and all they meet: that You, God, have given them eternal life, and this life is lived out in Your Son. Grow them in grace and knowledge of our Lord and Savior. Pour out grace on them abundantly, along with the faith and love that come by believing in Him. Break every enslaving yoke in their lives as they grow to maturity. This will be to Your glory: that these grandchildren bear much fruit in their lives, showing themselves to be disciples of Jesus Christ. Thank You that Jesus stands at the door of their hearts and knocks, and if my grandchildren hear and listen to and heed His Voice and open the door, He will come in to them and will eat with them, and they will eat with Jesus. May my grandchildren bring honor to You, recognizing that Jesus is the Name above all names and He is the Lord of all. I pray this in the Name of Your Son, the Messiah. Amen.

(2 Tim. 2: 10; Matt. 10:32; 2 Tim. 1: 9; Phil. 2: 9; 1 John 5: 11;
2 Peter 3: 18; 1 Tim. 1: 14; John 15:8; Rev. 3: 20)

Father, as I sit quietly before You praying for my grandchildren, is there any word, Scripture, insight, or particular situation related to salvation which concerns my grandchildren that You want to bring to my heart? I surrender my thoughts to You and I commit to pray in obedience to what You reveal.

Word:

Date:

Sealed

Heavenly Father, my grandchildren have "my seal of approval." They bring me joy and gratefulness, and I approve of them unconditionally. Even greater than their grandparent's approval, they have an astonishing blessing: You mark my grandchildren as Your very own possession. You set Your seal of ownership on my grandchildren and put Your Spirit in their hearts as a deposit, guaranteeing what is to come. Your Presence in their hearts guarantees their redemption and is for the praise of Your glory. Thank You for the blessed ministry of sanctification in their lives which will cause them to be transformed into the likeness of our dearest Lord Jesus, reflecting His glory in the world. Because of Your Spirit, my grandchildren will not set their life's work for the food that spoils. The Spirit will lead them to strive and work for the food that endures which Jesus will give them. You will place Your seal of approval on them. They will receive the sign of circumcision (a circumcision of the heart), a seal of righteousness. It will be a credit to those who believe. In faith, I believe that when my grandchildren hear the word of truth, the gospel of their salvation, they will believe it, and they will be marked in Jesus with a seal, the promised Holy Spirit. To You Who sits on the Throne, my heavenly Father, and to the Son, the Lamb of God slain for my sin, I ascribe praise, honor, glory, and power forever. Amen.

(John 6: 27; Rom 4: 11; 2 Cor. 1:22; Eph. 1: 13)

Father, as I sit quietly before You praying for my grandchildren, is there any word, Scripture, insight, or particular situation related to this topic which concerns my grandchildren that You want to bring to my heart? I surrender my thoughts to You and I commit to pray in obedience to what You reveal.

Word:

Date:

Truth - 1

Father, I pray that my grandchildren will be lovers of the truth. So many philosophies and world views call to them. I pray my grandchildren's minds will be conformed not to this world, but bound to the Mind of Christ. May they hold to Your teaching, may they really be Your disciples, then they will know the Truth and the Truth will set them free. May Your Spirit hover over their lives, and may Your Spirit guide them into all truth. Sanctify my grandchildren by the truth. Your Word is truth. May they know that the Word became flesh and made His dwelling among us. May they know that Jesus said, "I am the Way and the Truth and the Life. No one comes to the Father, except through Me." I know that the coming of the lawless one will be in accordance with the work of Satan displayed in all kinds of counterfeit miracles, signs, wonders, and in every sort of evil that deceives those who are perishing. They perish because they refuse to love the truth and so be saved. Convict my grandchildren that Your Word is the Truth and Christ is the Word. He reveals Himself only to those who hold to His teachings. May they never be deceived into thinking that the Word of God is not the only way to the Father. Sanctify them through the ministry of the Holy Spirit through the Word. I pray this in Jesus' Name. Amen.

(John 8: 31–32; John 16: 13; John 17;17; John 14: 6; John 1: 1, 14; 2 Thess. 2: 9, 10)

Father, as I sit quietly before You praying for my grandchildren, is there any word, Scripture, insight, or particular situation related to this topic which concerns my grandchildren that You want to bring to my heart? I surrender my thoughts to You and I commit to pray in obedience to what You reveal.

Word:

Date:

Truth - 2

Father, today's culture tells my grandchildren that there is no truth; everything is relative. I proclaim that You are the Truth. I pray that You will keep my grandchildren's minds ever renewed by Your Word and they will know the truth. May they base their lives on Your truth instead of Satan's lies, so that they will experience all the freedom that Jesus died to give them. I pray that they will set their thoughts on what is true, noble, right, pure, lovely admirable, excellent, and worthy of praise. I pray that they will not conform to the pattern of this world, but will be transformed by the renewing of their minds. Then they will be able to test and approve what God's will is—Your good, pleasing and perfect will. *"Then they will know the truth, and the truth will set them free."* I pray this in Jesus' Name. Amen.

(John 8:32; Phil 4: 8; Rom. 12: 2)

Father, as I sit quietly before You praying for my grandchildren, is there any word, Scripture, insight, or particular situation related to truth which concerns my grandchildren that You want to bring to my heart? I surrender my thoughts to You and I commit to pray in obedience to what You reveal.

Word:

Date:

Voice of the Lord

Almighty God, Heavenly Father, I pray for my grandchildren to be obedient to Your Voice. Whether they turn to the right or to the left, may their ears hear Your Voice behind them, saying, "This is the way; walk in it." Let the Holy Spirit say to my grandchildren: "Today, if you hear the Father's Voice, do not harden your hearts." For You are their God and my grandchildren are the people of Your pasture and the sheep of Your hand. Today, if they hear Your voice, help them not to harden their hearts, for You are their God forever and ever; You will be their guide even until death. You will bring the blind by a way that they do not know, in paths that they have not known. You will make darkness into light before them and make uneven places into a plain. These things You have determined to do for them; and You will not leave them forsaken. When the Holy Spirit, the Spirit of Truth comes, He will guide my grandchildren into the whole, full Truth. He will not speak His own message on His own authority; but He will tell whatever He hears from the Father; He will give the message that has been given to Him, and He will announce and declare to my grandchildren the things that are to come. May they give ear to Your words, O Lord. Make their ears attentive to skillful and godly Wisdom and incline and direct their hearts and minds to understanding, so that they will apply all their powers in their quest for You. It is written: "No eye has seen, no ear has heard, no mind has conceived what God has prepared for those who love Him." Open my grandchildren's ears to receive this amazing promise through the power and Voice of Your Holy Spirit. Amen.

(Is. 30: 21; Heb. 3: 7; Ps. 95: 7- 10; Ps. 48:14; Is. 42: 16; John 16: 13; Prov 2: 2; 1 Cor. 2: 9 NIV)

Father, as I sit quietly before You praying for my grandchildren, is there any word, Scripture, insight, or particular situation related to this topic which concerns my grandchildren that You want to bring to my heart? I surrender my thoughts to You and I commit to pray in obedience to what You reveal.

Word:

Date:

The Word - 1

Heavenly Father, I pray for my grandchildren–those now known to me and those whom You will bring to my family in the future. Jesus, Who is infinite wisdom and knowledge, will not hesitate to come down to my grandchildren to be their Guide and Master. Do not permit them to be so foolish as to forget You. May they always listen to Your Word and continually seek Your light and strength. Your Word is such an important part of my life, I pray that it will be the same for my grandchildren and that it will be living and sharper than any two-edged sword in their lives, piercing even to the division of their souls and spirits, discerning the thoughts and intents of their hearts. May my grandchildren never forget that the Word of God endures forever. Give my grandchildren a hunger to know Your Word, O Lord, and to meditate on it day and night. Let it be a lamp to their feet and a light to their path. Give them boldness to proclaim it. I pray that my grandchildren will put into practice the truth that they cannot live by bread alone, but by every Word that proceeds from Your mouth. I pray that my grandchildren will always understand and apply the truth that all Scripture is given by Your inspiration and is profitable for doctrine, for reproof, for correction, and for instruction in righteousness, that they may be complete and thoroughly equipped for every good work. I pray that my grandchildren will take to heart that heaven and earth will pass away, but Your Word will by no means ever pass away. In Jesus' Name, Amen.

(Hebrews 4:12; 1 Peter 1: 25; Joshua 1:8; Ps. 119:105; Matt. 4:4)

Father, as I sit quietly before You praying for my grandchildren, is there any word, Scripture, insight, or particular situation related to this topic which concerns my grandchildren that You want to bring to my heart? I surrender my thoughts to You and I commit to pray in obedience to what You reveal.

Word:

Date:

The Word - 2

Heavenly Father, I pray that my grandchildren will be born again, not from a mortal origin but from one that is immortal by the ever living and lasting Word of God. For truly You have told us, until the sky and earth pass away and perish, not one small letter nor one little hook [identifying certain Hebrew letters] will pass from the Law until all things it foreshadows are accomplished. I pray that if my grandchildren will abide in Your Word, if they will hold fast to Your teachings and live in accordance with them, they will truly be Your disciples. And they will know the Truth, and the Truth will set them free. Help my grandchildren learn the significance of Your promise: "It is the same with My Word. I send it out, and it always produces fruit. It will accomplish all I want it to, and it will prosper everywhere I send it." I stand on Your Word that Your Spirit will not leave them, and neither will the words You have given them. Your words will be on the lips of my children and my children's children forever. They will meditate on it day and night, so that they may observe and do according to what is written in it. For then You will make their way prosperous, and then they will deal wisely with others and have good success. May my grandchildren take Your testimonies as a heritage forever, for they are the rejoicing of their hearts. I pray, God, that You will instruct my grandchildren in the way they should go, and You will guide them with Your eye. In Jesus' Name, I pray. Amen.

(1 Peter 1: 23; Matt 5:18; John 8: 31–32; Is 55:11; Joshua 1:8; Is. 59: 21; Ps. 119:111; Ps. 32:8)

Father, as I sit quietly before You praying for my grandchildren, is there any word, Scripture, insight, or particular situation related to this topic which concerns my grandchildren that You want to bring to my heart? I surrender my thoughts to You and I commit to pray in obedience to what You reveal.

Word:

Date:

Word of God - 3
Choosing Holiness over Evil

Heavenly Father, I pray for my precious grandchildren this day–those that are known and those who have not yet been born. You know all of them, Lord God, because Your Word tells us that Your eyes see their unformed substance, and in Your book all the days of their lives were written before they ever took shape, when as yet there was not one of them. I beseech You to write Your Word on the hearts of my grandchildren. Young men and women will cleanse their way and have lives of purity if they take heed and keep watch according to what Your Word teaches. May my grandchildren conform their lives to Your law. I pray that they will choose the obedience of hating sin and loving Your holiness. I pray that they will shun youthful lusts and flee from them, and aim at and pursue righteousness, faith, love, and harmony with others. May they be in fellowship with all Christians who call upon the Lord out of a pure heart. I would have them well versed and wise as to what is good and innocent, and guileless as to what is evil. Work in their lives the holy fear of a Living God and the righteousness of their Savior Jesus. Prevent them from simply keeping a set of rules, but desiring to please You in all they do. Create in them a pure heart. Make them wise in what is good, and innocent in what is evil. I pray this in Jesus' Name. Amen.

(Ps. 139: 16; Ps. 119:9; 2 Tim. 2: 22; Rom. 16: 19b; Prov. 8: 13)

Father, as I sit quietly before You praying for my grandchildren, is there any word, Scripture, insight, or particular situation related to this topic which concerns my grandchildren that You want to bring to my heart? I surrender my thoughts to You and I commit to pray in obedience to what You reveal.

Word:

Date:

Prayers for a Life that Honors God

Approval

Heavenly Father, children always look for favor with their peers. You have placed in them a need for community ~ for relationships where they can grow and share. Give them wisdom in distinguishing between the approval that pleases You and the approval that comes from pleasing a crowd. I ask for the type of friends that will serve as good role models for my grandchildren, and who will be safe and trustworthy. "As iron sharpens iron, a friend sharpens a friend." May my grandchildren experience friendships that challenge in a godly fashion. Keep them from comparing themselves to others all their lives. Deliver them from the traps of vanity and materialism. May they pursue holiness over outward beauty and material rewards. "For it is not the one who commends himself who is approved, but the one whom the Lord commends." "As for the rich in this world, charge them not to be proud and arrogant and contemptuous of others, nor to set their hopes on uncertain riches, but on You, Who richly and ceaselessly provide us with everything for our enjoyment."

The world will tempt them to attain and to boast. Others will urge them to participate in activities that bring temporary honor. Keep them from these temptations, Father. You say there are six things You hate, seven that are detestable to You. The first on that list is haughty eyes. May my grandchildren keep ever humble before You. For You save the humble but bring low those whose eyes are haughty. Keep my grandchildren's hearts from being proud, O LORD. Keep their eyes from haughtiness. May they not concern themselves with great matters or things too wonderful for them to comprehend that You have reserved for heaven alone. You guide the humble in what is right and teach them Your way. You take delight in Your people; You crown the humble with salvation. May my grandchildren keep ever humble before You, recognizing the condition of their hearts. Your Word instructs that they can choose to obey You and receive Your approval. The saints of old received Your approval because of their faith. May my grandchildren seek the approval that comes from You, the LORD their God, and not the approval that comes from man. Amen.

(Prov. 27: 17 NLT; 2 Cor. 10 :18 NIV; 1 Tim. 6: 17; Prov. 6: 17; Ps. 18: 27; Ps. 25: 9; Ps. 131: 1; Ps. 149: 4; Rom. 6: 16; Heb. 11: 2, 39)

Father, as I sit quietly before You praying for my grandchildren, is there any word, Scripture, insight, or particular situation related to seeking approval which concerns my grandchildren that You want to bring to my heart? I surrender my thoughts to You and I commit to pray in obedience to what You reveal.

Word:

Date:

Attachments

Heavenly Father, it is from my position as grandparent that I am able to look back and recognize that You are always desiring to break into my life in order to completely transform me into Your light and love. You have wanted to free me from my worldly attachments. I now have eyes to see that in proportion to my conforming my will to Your will, not only in serious matters but even in the smallest details of my life, the more capable I become of being transformed by Your divine grace. O God, my grandchildren have so many worldly pulls on their lives. Our society tells them that to be happy, they must "have" or "be" and "behave" in ways that are contrary to Your will for them. May they gain understanding at an early age that following You consists of detaching themselves from everything that is not You. Give them the light necessary to recognize all that keeps them from walking closely with their Lord. They will have great need of Your help, for they will become too attached to be capable of struggling against their misplaced affections, of giving up those little pleasures which feed "self." As is the condition of man, they will love themselves too much to sacrifice what brings separation from You. May my grandchildren be different! May they arrive at the understanding of loving You with their whole hearts, minds, and strength. Father, Your Word says You will examine their motives and the impurity of their hearts. You will create a clean heart in them. As they grow, with the empowerment of Your Holy Spirit, please grant them the desire to detach themselves from everything that might tether them to earth and not to You. Enable them to see that what they lose is nothing in comparison with the immense treasure You have purchased for them, an attachment to You, my God, You Who are All. In Jesus' Name, I pray. Amen.

(Psalm 51; 1 John 2: 15)

Father, as I sit quietly before You praying for my grandchildren, is there any word, Scripture, insight, or particular situation related to this topic which concerns my grandchildren that You want to bring to my heart? I surrender my thoughts to You and I commit to pray in obedience to what You reveal.

Word:

Date:

Called to Missions

Lord God, King of all the Earth, as my grandchildren get older, some will be called to serve You in the mission field. What an honor that will be! When that happens, it will be hard for me and my family to relinquish that grandchild to Your service in a part of the world that may present hardship and danger and separation. I will lean on Your Word to teach me how to release these grandchildren into Your arms. Your servants in Scripture demonstrated that there is no surrender apart from full surrender. My grandchildren were committed to You before they were even born. I have prayed they would know Jesus as Savior and Lord, that You would use them for Your glory. My highest aspiration is to see these children walk with You and be obedient to Your call on their lives. But when that time comes for them to launch out, I will be somewhat fearful. You promise that You have plans not to harm my grandchildren but to prosper them and bring them a hope and a future. Your highest good is that they will be conformed to the likeness of Your Son. As I send out my grandchildren to fulfill Your divine imperative to "Go and preach and baptize," help me cast all my concerns and worries on You. Bind my mind and desires to Your mind and will. Watch over my grandchildren, O Lord. I acknowledge they belong to You. You loan them to us for a short while to love, nurture, train, and prepare for the work set before them. Thank You for the opportunities You will provide them to participate in such a high calling. Build Your Kingdom on the earth. Every knee will bow and every tongue will confess that Jesus Christ is Lord. Thank You that my grandchildren will take the Gospel to the peoples of the earth. How beautiful are the feet of those who bring good news! In Jesus' Name, I pray. Amen.

(Acts 1: 8; Matt. 28: 19–20; Jer. 29: 11; Phil 2: 10–11, Romans 10: 15)

Father, as I sit quietly before You praying for my grandchildren, is there any word, Scripture, insight, or particular situation related to this topic on missions which concerns my grandchildren that You want to bring to my heart? I surrender my thoughts to You and I commit to pray in obedience to what You reveal.

Word:

Date:

Devoted Followers

Heavenly Father, thank You that You are causing my grandchildren to examine what it means to be fully devoted disciples of Jesus Christ. Thank You for sanctifying them by Your Word which is truth. Jesus consecrated Himself for our sake, so we will be truth-consecrated in our mission. Help my grandchildren to always repent and turn from any wicked ways. May they cease to do evil, and learn to do right. *(John 17: 17,19; Is. 1: 16,17)*

Father, You dwell in my grandchildren. May they leave corruption and compromise; may they leave it for good. You are their Father; You want them for Yourself. Prevent them from linking up with those who will pollute them. May they purify themselves from everything that contaminates the body and spirit, perfecting holiness out of a reverential fear of Your righteousness. *(2 Cor. 7:1)*

May they confess their sins. You are faithful and just to forgive sins and to cleanse them from all unrighteousness. Jesus has been made to them wisdom, sanctification, and redemption. May they submit themselves to You ~ spirit, soul, and body. May they strip themselves of their old, unrenewed selves which characterized their previous behavior. May they put on the new nature, changing whatever needs to be corrected in their lives. May the desire of their hearts be to become vessels You can use for Your purpose. Then they will be ready for the Master to use for every good work. *(1 John 1:9; 1 Cor. 1:30; Eph. 4: 22–24; 2 Tim. 2:21)*

May my grandchildren commend themselves in every way as Your true servants. They will need great endurance in tribulation and suffering, in hardships and privations, in sore straits and calamities, in beatings, imprisonments, riots, labors, sleepless watching, and hunger. May they reflect innocence and purity, knowledge and spiritual insight, longsuffering, patience, and kindness, through the Holy Spirit, in sincere love. May they speak the Word of Truth, in Your power, with the weapons of righteousness for the right hand to attack and the left hand to defend. *(2 Cor. 6: 4–7)*

Thank You, Lord, that my grandchildren can eat the good of the land, because You have given them willing and obedient hearts. *(Is. 1:19)*

I pray this in Jesus' Name. Amen.

Father, as I sit quietly before You praying for my grandchildren, is there any word, Scripture, insight, or particular situation related to this topic which concerns my grandchildren that You want to bring to my heart? I surrender my thoughts to You and I commit to pray in obedience to what You reveal.

Word:

Date:

Doers of the Word - 2 Timothy 2

Heavenly Father, as I pray for my grandchildren today, I pray that they will be young people who will always concentrate on doing their best for You, work they will not be ashamed of, correctly laying out the truth. I pray that they will stay clear of pious talk that is only talk, for words are not mere words. They carry power. If they are not backed by a godly life, these empty words accumulate as poison in the soul. Your firm foundation is as firm as ever; these sentences are engraved on the stones:

"GOD KNOWS WHO BELONGS TO HIM. SPURN EVIL ALL YOU WHO NAME GOD AS GOD."

Your Word tells us that in a well-furnished kitchen there are not only crystal goblets and silver platters, but waste cans and compost buckets ~ some containers used to serve fine meals, others to take out garbage. I pray that my grandchildren will become the kind of vessel You can use to present any and every kind of gift to guests for their blessing. I pray that as my grandchildren grow, they will run away from childish indulgence, and will run after mature righteousness ~ faith, love, peace ~ joining those who are in honest and serious prayer before You. Help them to refrain from getting involved in inane discussions that always end up in contention. As Your servants, may they keep from being argumentative, but become gentle listeners and teachers who remain at peace, working firmly but patiently with those who refuse to obey. May they be able to discern how or when You might convict a companion with a change of heart and a turning to the truth. Enable them to escape the devil's trap, where they are caught and held captive, forced to run his errands. May my grandchildren know that this is a sure thing: if they die with Jesus, they will live with Him; if they stand with Jesus, they will rule with Him; if they turn their backs on Jesus, He will turn His back on them; if they give up on Him, He does not give up ~ for there is no way He can be false to Himself. May they repeat these basic essentials over and over to God's people. I pray for my grandchildren this day to be people who are doers of the Word and not simply hearers. In Jesus' Name, Amen.

Father, as I sit quietly before You praying for my grandchildren, is there any word, Scripture, insight, or particular situation related to this topic which concerns my grandchildren that You want to bring to my heart? I surrender my thoughts to You and I commit to pray in obedience to what You reveal.

Word:

Date:

Drink

Almighty God, You have said that if anyone thirsts, he can come to You and drink. I pray that my grandchildren's souls will long, yea, even faint for Your courts. May their hearts and their flesh cry out and sing for joy to the living God. O God, You are their God; earnestly will they seek You. May their souls thirst for You; may their flesh long for You in a dry and thirsty land where there is no water. May they look for You in the sanctuary to see Your power and Your glory. Let my grandchildren thirst and be painfully conscious of their need of those things which refresh, support, and strengthen the soul; and may they earnestly desire You, and take the water of life freely. Call to them, O God, and say, "Eat, O friends! Drink, yes, drink deeply, O beloved ones." May my grandchildren drink of the water that You will give to them and they shall never, no never, be thirsty again. And the water You will give them shall become a spring of water welling up, flowing, bubbling continually within them into eternal life. This I pray, in Jesus' Name. Amen.

(John 7: 37; Ps. 84: 2; Ps. 63:1–2; Rev. 22: 17b; SS 5: 1e; John 4: 12–14)

Father, as I sit quietly before You praying for my grandchildren, is there any word, Scripture, insight, or particular situation related to this topic which concerns my grandchildren that You want to bring to my heart? I surrender my thoughts to You and I commit to pray in obedience to what You reveal.

Word:

Date:

Faithful Witnesses

Lord God, I know that in this generation, my grandchildren will be ridiculed for sharing their faith openly. For that reason, I pray that they will be bold witnesses for You despite persecution. May Your Word be strong in their hearts, like a burning fire shut up in their bones. Let it so consume them that they will grow weary from holding it back, and they will speak powerfully of Your Truth. For preaching the Good News is not something they can boast about. You compel them to do it. How terrible for them if they hold back! If they were doing this of their own free will, then they would deserve payment. But You have chosen my grandchildren and given them this sacred trust, and they have no choice. What then is their pay? It is the satisfaction they will get from preaching the Good News without expense to anyone, never demanding their rights as a witness. May they reply like Peter and John saying, "We cannot but speak the things which we have seen and heard. The love of Jesus compels us." May they go to their friends and tell them what great things the Lord has done in their own lives. I pray this in the Name of Your Son. Amen.

(Jer. 20: 9; 1 Cor. 9: 16–18; Acts 4: 18–20; 2 Cor. 5: 14; Mark 5: 19)

Father, as I sit quietly before You praying for my grandchildren, is there any word, Scripture, insight, or particular situation related to this topic which concerns my grandchildren that You want to bring to my heart? I surrender my thoughts to You and I commit to pray in obedience to what You reveal.

Word:

Date:

God is Jealous

Adapted from a Charles Spurgeon meditation

Thank You, Father, that You are very jealous of my grandchildren's love. You chose them. You cannot bear that they should choose another. You bought them with Jesus' own blood. You cannot endure that they would think that they are their own, or that they belong to this world.

You loved my grandchildren with such a love that You would not stop in heaven without them; You would sooner sacrifice the life of Your Son rather than they should perish, and You cannot endure that anything would stand between their hearts' love and Yourself. You are very jealous of their trust. You will not permit my grandchildren to trust in an arm of flesh.

You cannot bear that they should hew out broken cisterns when the overflowing fountain is always free to them. When my grandchildren lean upon You, You are glad; but when they transfer their dependence to another, when they rely upon their own wisdom, or the wisdom of a friend, when they trust in any works of their own, You are displeased, and will chasten them that so that You may bring them to Yourself.

You are also very jealous of their company. There should be no one with whom my grandchildren converse so much as with Jesus. Help them to abide in Him only, for this is true love. Keep them from communing with the world, from finding sufficient solace in its carnal comforts, from preferring even the friendship of their fellow Christians to secret communion with You. I know this is grievous to You, jealous Lord. You would have my grandchildren abide in Jesus, and enjoy constant fellowship with Yourself. Many of the trials which You send them are for the purpose of weaning their hearts from others, and fixing them more closely on Yourself.

Let this jealousy which would keep my grandchildren near to Christ be also a comfort to them, for if You love them so much as to care about their unencumbered love, I may be sure that You will let nothing harm them, and will protect them from all their enemies. O, that my grandchildren may have grace each day to keep their hearts in sacred chastity for You, my Beloved Lord, with sacred jealousy shutting their eyes to all the fascinations of the world! In Jesus' Name, I pray. Amen.

(Nahum 1: 2; Exodus 20: 5; Deut. 5: 9; Jer. 2: 13; Acts 20: 28)

Father, as I sit quietly before You praying for my grandchildren, is there any word, Scripture, insight, or particular situation related to this topic which concerns my grandchildren that You want to bring to my heart? I surrender my thoughts to You and I commit to pray in obedience to what You reveal.

Word:

Date:

God - Minded, Spirit - Led

Father, I pray that my grandchildren will be God-minded and Spirit-led. I know that they live in this world, but are not of it. They will walk through the corruption and degradation of this age while You make them holy in every way. May their spirits and souls and bodies be kept blameless. Because they proclaim Jesus as Lord, they are Your children, born of the Spirit of God, filled with Spirit of God, and led by the Spirit of God. You have given them the promised Holy Spirit to direct them. He will guide my grandchildren into all truth. Your Word says that the Spirit will not be operating from His own thoughts; He reveals only what He has heard from You, the Father. Jesus said, "I assure you, the Son can do nothing by Himself. He does only what he sees the Father doing. Whatever the Father does, the Son also does." The Spirit also serves at Your beckoning, Lord. You instruct Him to penetrate human spirits with a holy searchlight, exposing every hidden motive. Because You actually indwell my grandchildren through Your Spirit, they are able to listen to Your Voice speaking in their hearts the wonderful promises available to them. Thank You, Holy Spirit, for directing my grandchildren and illuminating their minds. You will always lead them in ways they should go in every concern. The eyes of their understanding are being enlightened in order to understand the hope to which they have been called. They have an anointing from You, the Holy One. You give them an inward witness, encouraging them to appropriate the power and promises available to their lives. Help them to obey what the Spirit tells them. May they examine their leadings in light of the Word and with the affirmation of the Body of Christ. They will need to trust in You, Lord, with all of their hearts and lean not to their own understanding. In all their ways may they acknowledge You, and You will direct their paths. May they walk in light of their understanding of the Word. May the Holy Spirit be their counselor, training their spirits and prompting their obedience. May they grow to understand these things, for my grandchildren will have the Mind of Christ. Thank You, Lord, for these great mercies. In Jesus' Name, I pray. Amen.

(1 Thess. 5: 23; John 16:13; John 5: 19 NLT; Prov. 20:27;
1 Cor. 2: 12; Rom. 8:14,16; John 3:6,7; Is. 48:17; Eph.1: 18;
1 John 2: 20; Prov. 3: 5,6; Ps. 119: 105; John 14: 26;
1 Cor. 2: 16)

Father, as I sit quietly before You praying for my grandchildren, is there any word, Scripture, insight, or particular situation related to this topic which concerns my grandchildren that You want to bring to my heart? I surrender my thoughts to You and I commit to pray in obedience to what You reveal.

Word:

Date:

Good Soil

Father, I thank You that my children and grandchildren are good soil, that they will hear Your Word for them and understand it, and that it will bear fruit in their lives - sometimes a hundredfold, sometimes sixty, sometimes thirty. They are planted by rivers of water that bring forth fruit in season. Their leaf will not wither, and whatever they do will prosper. In Jesus' Name, I thank You for filling them with the knowledge of Your will in all wisdom and spiritual understanding, that they may walk worthy of You, being fruitful in good works and increasing in their knowledge of You. Lord, would you seal all knowledge gained through my grandchildren's early lives and experiences. Would you imprint on their hearts the lessons they learn for their own walks of faith. And would you cut from my grandchildren any remembrances that would cause them to stumble, sealing only those memories that would edify and grow them fully into Your purposes. Thank You for extraordinary adventures that they will experience throughout their childhoods and teenage years in the power of Your Son. Bring them up safely, girded by Your incredible work in their lives. In the Name of Your Son, I pray. Amen.

(Matt. 13: 23; Ps. 1:3; Col. 1:10)

Father, as I sit quietly before You praying for my grandchildren, is there any word, Scripture, insight, or particular situation related to my grandchildren being good soil that You want to bring to my heart? I surrender my thoughts to You and I commit to pray in obedience to what You reveal.

Word:

Date:

Honesty

LORD, you are searching for honesty. You desire honesty from the heart. You will teach my grandchildren to be wise in their inmost being. You hate cheating, but You delight in honesty. I pray that my grandchildren will always tell the truth. They may momentarily be tempted to lie for self-protection, but they will yield to Your Spirit. Integrity and honesty will bring protection, for they put their hope in You. Teach them how to live, O LORD. Lead them along the path of honesty, for their enemies are waiting for them to fall. Yes, what joy for those whose record the LORD has cleared of sin, whose lives are lived in complete honesty! You paint a clear distinction. Good people are guided by their honesty; treacherous people are destroyed by their dishonesty. The godly are directed by their honesty; the wicked fall beneath their load of sin. Keep them from lying, Lord God. May only truth come from their lips. In Jesus' Name, I pray. Amen.

(Jer. 5: 3; Ps. 51: 6; Ps. 25: 21; Ps. 27: 10; Ps. 32: 2;
Prov. 11: 1;5 NLT)

Father, as I sit quietly before You praying for my grandchildren, is there any word, Scripture, insight, or particular situation related to this topic which concerns my grandchildren that You want to bring to my heart? I surrender my thoughts to You and I commit to pray in obedience to what You reveal.

Word:

Date:

Humble Life

I pray, Lord God, that my grandchildren will take their confidence from You and not from any self conceit. May they know that You are the One Who has given them life and endowed them with the wonderful attributes they possess. I pray that if my grandchildren glory, they will glory only in You. For in their pride, they will not seek You; in all their self-directed thoughts, there is no room for You. You, Lord, ask my grandchildren, "Should you then seek great things for yourself? Seek them not." May they not exalt themselves in the king's presence, nor claim a place among great men. May they learn that it is better for a nobleman to say to them, "Come up here," than to be humiliated by not being invited. May they take on the character of Christ and become people who do nothing out of selfish ambition or vain conceit, but in humility consider others better than themselves. Grant that they will look not only to their own interests, but also to the interests of others. May they learn that it is not good to eat too much honey, nor is it honorable to seek one's own honor. For whoever exalts himself will be humbled, and whoever humbles himself will be exalted. May they learn not to accept praise from another, while making no effort to obtain the praise that comes from the Living God. For if in their own eyes they flatter themselves, it will be hard to detect or hate their own sin. May they examine their ways and test them, and may they always return to You, Lord. I pray that my grandchildren will draw near to You and put their trust in the LORD that they may declare all Your works. I pray that my grandchildren will delight themselves in You, and You will give them the desires of their hearts. In Jesus' Name, Amen.

(1 Cor. 1: 31; Ps. 10: 4; Jer. 45: 5 NIV; Prov 25: 6–7; Phil 2: 3;
Prov. 25: 27; Matt 23: 12; John 5: 44; Ps. 36: 2; Lam 3: 40;
Ps. 73: 28)

Father, as I sit quietly before You praying for my grandchildren, is there any word, Scripture, insight, or particular situation related to this topic which concerns my grandchildren that You want to bring to my heart? I surrender my thoughts to You and I commit to pray in obedience to what You reveal.

Word:

Date:

In the Center of God's Will

Heavenly Father, more than anything else I desire that my grandchildren live godly lives in Your sight. Your words are my prayers to You on their behalf. Please honor them by keeping my grandchildren in the center of Your will in all that they do. God, in accordance with Your Word, I pray that if my grandchildren live, they live to please the Lord. And if they die, they go to be with the Lord. So in life and in death, they belong to the Lord. I pray that they will give their bodies to You. Let them be a living and holy sacrifice ~ the kind You will accept. When they think of what You have done for them, this is not too much to ask. Keep them from copying the behaviors and customs of this world, but transform them into new persons by changing the way they think. Then they will know what You require of them. I pray that by Your grace they will be honest in their estimate of themselves. I pray that they will not have an exaggerated opinion of their own importance, but will rate their ability with sober judgment, each measuring their value by how much faith You have given them. I hold claim that my grandchildren will be counted among those whom You foreordained and You have also called; and those whom You called, You will also justify. I stand on the promise that when You justify my grandchildren, You promise them Your glory. Therefore, may my grandchildren know that if any person is engrafted in Christ the Messiah, he is a new creation (a new creature altogether); the old, previous moral and spiritual condition has passed away. Behold, the fresh and new has come! I pray this in the Name of Your Son. Amen.

(Rom. 14: 8; Rom. 12: 1–3; Rom 8: 30; 2 Cor. 5: 17)

Father, as I sit quietly before You praying for my grandchildren, is there any word, Scripture, insight, or particular situation related to this topic which concerns my grandchildren that You want to bring to my heart? I surrender my thoughts to You and I commit to pray in obedience to what You reveal.

Word:

Date:

Knowing God

Thank You, Father, that my grandchildren can know You, the one true God, intimately. Thank You that they can apply all Your Names. How majestic is Your Name in all the earth! You have never forsaken those who seek You. Your Name is a strong tower. My grandchildren, who are made righteous, will run to You and be safe.

You are **Jehovah Elohim**, dependable, faithful, and strong to my grandchildren. *Exo. 3: 14–17; Heb. 13: 8*

You are **Jehovah Shaddai**, mighty and more than enough for them. *Exo. 6:3; Eph. 3: 20–21*

You are **Jehovah Adonai,** their Master and Sovereign Lord. *2 Sam 7: 17–29; James 4: 11–17*

You are **Jehovah Jireh**, their Source, Provider, and Sustainer. *Gen. 22: 14; Phil. 4: 19*

You are **Jehovah Rophe,** my grandchildren's Healer. *Ex. 15: 22–27; Is. 53: 5; Matt. 8: 16–17; 1 Peter 2: 24*

You are **Jehovah Nissi**, their Banner, Standard, and Victory. *Ex. 17: 15–16; 1 Cor. 15: 57; 2 Cor. 2: 14*

You are **Jehovah Rohi,** their Shepherd and Protector. *Ps. 23; John 10; Heb. 13: 20; 1 Peter 5: 4*

You are **Jehovah Shalom.** The Lord is their Peace.
Judges 6: 24; Is. 26: 3–4; Rom. 5: 1; John 16: 33

You are **Jehovah Tsidkenu,** their Righteousness and Redemption.
Jer. 23: 5,6; Rom. 3: 22–25; 2 Cor. 5: 21

You are **Jehovah Shammah**, the Lord Who is present, faithful, and always with my grandchildren.
Eze. 48: 35; Matt. 28: 18–20; Heb. 13: 5,6

You are **Jehovah M'Kaddesh**, the Lord Who sanctifies. You are their Holiness.
Ex. 31: 13; Heb. 2: 10–11, 3: 1; 1 Peter 2: 9; Lev. 20: 7,8

You are **Jehovah Sabboath**, the Lord of Hosts, Commander of the angelic army. *Jos.5: 13–15; Heb. 1: 1–9*

You are **Jehovah Elyon**, my grandchildren's exaltation. You are the Most High God. *Ps. 7: 1, 17; Phil. 2: 5–11*

You are **Jehovah Hosenu,** their Creator and Maker.
Is. 45: 11; Col. 1: 15–20

Father, as my grandchildren grow, they will know Your name and will experience Your mercy. They will lean on and confidently put their trust in You, for You, Lord, have not forsaken those who inquire of and seek You. I pray that my grandchildren will seek You with all their hearts, and they will rely on Your character, on Your Name, in all their needs. May my grandchildren, who know their God, prove themselves strong and stand firm. May their determined purpose be to know You, that they may progressively become more deeply and intimately acquainted with You, perceiving and recognizing and understanding the wonders of Your Person more strongly and more clearly. In Jesus' Name, I pray. Amen.

(Ps. 9:10; Ps. 8: 1; Prov. 18: 10; Dan. 11: 32b)

Light to the World

Heavenly Father, I pray that You will make my grandchildren a light to the world. May they lead lives of those native born to the Light. For the fruit, the effect, of the Light or the Spirit consists in every form of kindly goodness, uprightness of heart, and trueness of life. May my grandchildren learn what is pleasing to You and may their lives be constant proofs of what is most acceptable to You. Let their hands bring You glory, and their thoughts and words give You honor. In Jesus' Name, even in their youth, may my grandchildren set an example for all believers in their speech, conduct, life, love, faith, and purity. In everything, may they set an example by doing what is good. In their lives, may they show integrity, seriousness, and soundness of speech that cannot be condemned, so that those who oppose them may be ashamed because they have nothing bad to say about my grandchildren. May my grandchildren show themselves to be wise and understanding among others. Let them show this by their good lives and by deeds done in the humility that comes from wisdom. May they have this wisdom that comes from heaven which is pure, peace-loving, considerate, submissive, full of mercy and good fruit, impartial, and sincere. I pray this in Jesus' Name. Amen.

(Eph. 5:8–10; 1 Tim. 4: 12; Titus 1: 7–8; James 3: 13, 17)

Father, as I sit quietly before You praying for my grandchildren, is there any word, Scripture, insight, or particular situation related to this topic which concerns my grandchildren that You want to bring to my heart? I surrender my thoughts to You and I commit to pray in obedience to what You reveal.

Word:

Date:

Obedience to Authority

Heavenly Father, this generation in large measure does not fear You. We have become a society which does not revere You or those You have placed in authority. For that reason, my grandchildren will need to know Your Word regarding obedience and submission to authority. I ask that You keep my grandchildren free from any rebellious spirit or attitude, especially in their teenage years. Your Word does not go out and return to You void, but it accomplishes what You say it will do, so I pray Your Word over my grandchildren. I pray that my grandchildren will obey those who rule over them, that they will be submissive, for their parents and teachers watch out for their souls as those who must give an account. Grant that my grandchildren may show proper respect to everyone as Your Word commands. Would You help them to listen to Your inner Voice, so that they can be taught the fear of the Lord. May they listen to their fathers, who gave them life, and not despise their mothers when they are old. May they honor their fathers and mothers, and obey their parents in the Lord, for this is right ~ and this is the first commandment with a promise ~ that if they are obedient to their parents, it will go well with them and they will enjoy long life on the earth. May my own sons and daughters train up my grandchildren in the way they should go; and then when my grandchildren are old, they will not depart from Your ways. May my grandchildren serve as godly examples to their peers as they obey their parents in the Lord as Your representatives. This is just and right according to Your commands. I believe and confess that my grandchildren will choose life and love You, Lord; they will obey Your voice and cling to You; for You are their Life and the Length of their days. The result will be that my grandchildren will be head and not the tail, and they shall be above only and not beneath. They will be blessed when they come in and when they go out. Help them obediently listen to and diligently keep Your commands to obey. In Jesus' Name, Amen.

(Eph. 6: 1–3; Deut. 28: 3, 6, 13; Deut. 30: 19, 20; 1 Sam. 15:23;
Heb. 13:17; 1 Peter 2: 13–14, 17; Ps. 34: 11; Prov. 23: 22;
Eph 6: 1–3; Prov. 22:6)

Father, as I sit quietly before You praying for my grandchildren, is there any word, Scripture, insight, or particular situation related to this topic which concerns my grandchildren that You want to bring to my heart? I surrender my thoughts to You and I commit to pray in obedience to what You reveal.

Word:

Date:

Paths

Father, let my grandchildren trust in You with all their hearts. In all their ways may You be acknowledged and therefore their paths be made straight. May they desire, God, to be on Your path. The path of the righteous is level. You make the way of the righteous smooth and just. You will guide them in the way of wisdom and lead them along straight paths. May my grandchildren say, "My steps have held to your paths; my feet have not slipped." Show them Your ways, O LORD, teach them Your paths of life. May they walk in the ways of good men and keep to the paths of the righteous. For a man's ways are in full view of the LORD, and You examine all his paths. Fasten their feet in shackles; keep close watch on all their paths. Whether they turn to the right or to the left, may their ears hear a Voice behind them, saying, "This is the way; walk in it." In Jesus' Name, I pray. Amen.

(Is. 26: 7; Ps. 16:11; Prov. 15:24; Heb 12:13; Is. 30: 21)

Father, as I sit quietly before You praying for my grandchildren, is there any word, Scripture, insight, or particular situation related to this topic which concerns my grandchildren that You want to bring to my heart? I surrender my thoughts to You and I commit to pray in obedience to what You reveal.

Word:

Date:

Peace

Most Gracious Father, I pray for my grandchildren today, that they will depart from evil and do good. May they always seek peace. May they pursue peace with all their hearts. When their ways please You, You make even their enemies at peace with them.

Lord, You have given my grandchildren Your peace; Your own peace You have bequeathed to them. It is not the peace that the world gives. Do not let their hearts be troubled, neither let them be afraid. May my grandchildren refuse to be agitated and disturbed. May they not allow themselves to be fearful and intimidated and cowardly and unsettled.

Instead of worrying, may my grandchildren know it is far better to pray. May they let their petitions and praises shape their worries into prayers, letting You, Father, know their concerns, not forgetting to thank You for the answers. May they keep Your peace in their thoughts and their hearts quiet and at rest as they learn to trust in Jesus Christ, their Lord. Wonderful things happen when Jesus displaces worry at the center of their lives.

Thank You for guarding my grandchildren and keeping them in perfect and constant peace. I claim that their minds, both in inclination and character, will be stayed on You. I pray they will commit themselves to You, lean on You, and hope confidently in You. Let the peace and harmony that comes from Jesus rule in their hearts, deciding and settling with finality all questions that arise in their minds. I am so grateful and appreciative that You will answer these prayers, and I give praise to You always. In Jesus' name, I pray. Amen.

(Prov. 16: 7; Ps. 34: 14; John 14: 27; 2 Peter 1: 2)

Father, as I sit quietly before You praying for my grandchildren, is there any word, Scripture, insight, or particular situation related to peace which concern my grandchildren that You want to bring to my heart? I surrender my thoughts to You and I commit to pray in obedience to what You reveal.

Word:

Date:

Personal Holiness

Father, please give my grandchildren deep conviction and commitment to personal holiness. They are Your temple, the abode of Your Spirit. I pray that they will remain pure and innocent in Your eyes. Lead them in the paths of righteousness, and give them power to resist temptation. May they spread truth in love and expose social injustice and prejudice of any kind. May Your Word be implanted in their hearts. May my grandchildren attend to Your Word, consent and submit to Your sayings. May Your statutes not depart from their sight; may they be kept in the center of their hearts. For Your words are life to those who find them; they are healing and health to their flesh. May my grandchildren keep and guard their hearts with all vigilance and above all that they guard, for out of their hearts flow the springs of life. May my grandchildren put away from them false and dishonest speech, and willful and contrary talk. May their eyes look with fixed purpose, and may their gaze be straight. May they consider well the path of their feet, and may all their ways be established and ordered aright. May they set their face like flint; may they not turn aside to the right hand or to the left; may they always remove their feet from evil. In Jesus' Name. Amen.

(Prov. 4: 20–27; Is. 50: 7)

Father, as I sit quietly before You praying for my grandchildren, is there any word, Scripture, insight, or particular situation related to this topic which concerns my grandchildren that You want to bring to my heart? I surrender my thoughts to You and I commit to pray in obedience to what You reveal.

Word:

Date:

Practicing Godliness

Heavenly Father, I pray that my grandchildren will be happy in their faith, and will rejoice and be glad-hearted always. May they be unceasing in prayer, thanking You in everything, no matter what the circumstances may be, for this is Your will for them who belong to Christ Jesus. I pray that they will not quench, stifle, or subdue the Holy Spirit. I pray that they will never scoff at the gifts and utterances of the prophets nor despise inspired instruction or exhortation or warning. Help them to test and prove all things until they can recognize what is good; to that may they hold fast. You will help them to abstain from evil in whatever form or whatever kind it may be. May You, the God of peace, sanctify my grandchildren through and through. Separate them from profane things, making my grandchildren pure and wholly consecrated to You. Father, may their spirits and souls and bodies be found blameless until that day when the Lord Jesus Christ comes again. You Who calls my grandchildren to Yourself are faithful; You are utterly trustworthy. You will do it ~ fulfill Your call ~ by sanctifying and keeping my grandchildren. Thank You and Amen.

(1 Thessalonians 5: 16–24)

Father, as I sit quietly before You praying for my grandchildren, is there any word, Scripture, insight, or particular situation related to this topic which concerns my grandchildren that You want to bring to my heart? I surrender my thoughts to You and I commit to pray in obedience to what You reveal.

Word:

Date:

Prayer

O Lord, You delight in the prayers of children. You have said, "Allow the children to come to Me ~ do not forbid or prevent or hinder them ~ for to such belongs the kingdom of God." I pray that my grandchildren will learn to communicate with You, not only to speak to You, but to hear Your Voice. They may start will small utterances, but as they grow, put Your praise on their hearts and on their lips continually. You have said, "have you never read, out of the mouths of babes and unweaned infants God has made perfect praise?" Lead them to be entirely dependent on You for everything so that they will talk with You about all their concerns. Father, my grandchildren will learn patience in prayer. They will need to persevere when their answers do not come at once. May they combine quiet patience with confident expectancy, for the power of believing prayer is considerable. You are anxious to give them what they ask. Your tender love longs to fully reveal itself by satisfying their desires. You will not delay a moment longer than is absolutely necessary to answer. How I thank You, Lord, that in my life and in theirs, Your infinite wisdom determines the times and seasons, the perfect moment when a soul is ready to receive and to appropriate the blessing of Your answer. Keep my grandchildren from thinking that a delayed response indicates an unwillingness to bless. They must learn that their prayers must agree with Your Word and Your character. Inspire their prayers by Your Holy Spirit, then their prayers will gain acceptance. Answer their prayers, Lord God, according to Your mercy and grace. I pray this in the Name of Jesus Christ. Amen.

(Mark 10: 14 TAB; Matt 21: 16; Phil 4: 8; Luke 11: 9; 1 John 5: 14)

Father, as I sit quietly before You praying for my grandchildren, is there any word, Scripture, insight, or particular situation related to prayer which concerns my grandchildren that You want to bring to my heart? I surrender my thoughts to You and I commit to pray in obedience to what You reveal.

Word:

Date:

Prayer Warrior

Dearest Lord, I pray that my grandchildren will become prayer warriors for You. I pray that they will devote themselves to prayer, being watchful and thankful. Before they even call, You, God, will answer; while they are still speaking, You will hear. You will hear them when they call to You. Teach them, as intercessors, to pray in the Spirit on all occasions, with all kinds of prayers and requests. May they be alert and always keep on praying for all the saints. May they not be anxious about anything, but in everything, by prayer and petition, with thanksgiving, present their requests to You. Out of Your glorious riches of love and power, You will fill these grandchildren with the desire and ability to grow in depth, insight, and frequency of prayer. Work in them through the ministry of the Holy Spirit so that they will become faithful, persistent, and complete in prayer. Make it the foundation of their lives. Unite them with Christ. In Him and in His Name they will have their confidence. Enable them to bear much eternal fruit for Jesus to the praise of His glorious grace. Burden my grandchildren with Your burdens and give Your vision of the power of prayer through which You will save the lost and build up Your church. By Your grace and mercy, enable my grandchildren to become prayer partners with the Savior, praying on earth as He is praying in heaven. In Jesus' Name and for His glory, I pray. Amen.

(Is. 65: 24; Ps. 4: 3; Col. 4: 2; Eph. 6: 18; Phil. 4: 6)

Father, as I sit quietly before You praying for my grandchildren, is there any word, Scripture, insight, or particular situation related to this topic on prayer which concern my grandchildren that You want to bring to my heart? I surrender my thoughts to You and I commit to pray in obedience to what You reveal.

Word:

Date:

Purity - Choosing Holiness over Evil

Heavenly Father, I pray for my precious grandchildren this day–those that are known and those who have not yet been born. You know all of them, Lord God, because Your Word tells me that Your eyes see their unformed substance, and in Your book all the days of their lives are written before they ever take shape, when as yet there is not one of them. I beseech You to write Your Word on the hearts of my grandchildren. For young men and women will cleanse their way and have lives of purity if they take heed and keep watch according to what Your Word teaches. May my grandchildren conform their lives to Your precepts. I pray that they will choose the obedience of hating sin and loving Your holiness. I pray that they will shun youthful lusts and flee from them, and aim at and pursue righteousness, faith, love, and harmony with others. May they be in fellowship with all Christians who call upon the Lord out of a pure heart. I would have them well versed and wise as to what is good and innocent, and guileless as to what is evil. Work in their lives the holy fear of Your Majesty and the righteousness of Jesus. Keep them from simply conforming to a set of rules, but stir in them a desire to please You in all they do. Create in them a pure heart. Make them wise in what is good, and innocent in what is evil. I pray this in Jesus' Name. Amen.

(Ps. 139: 16; Ps. 119:9; 2 Tim. 2: 22; Rom. 16: 19b; Prov. 8: 13)

Father, as I sit quietly before You praying for my grandchildren, is there any word, Scripture, insight, or particular situation related to this topic which concern my grandchildren that You want to bring to my heart? I surrender my thoughts to You and I commit to pray in obedience to what You reveal.

Word:

Date:

Rejoice Over

Father, when I think about my grandchildren, my heart smiles with delight. My grandchildren are Your creation. You delight over them in a way I cannot even imagine. You appeared from of old, saying, "Yes, I have loved you with an everlasting love; therefore with loving-kindness have I drawn you and continued My faithfulness to you." The steps of the godly are directed by the LORD. You delight in every detail of their lives. You bring Your children to the banqueting house, and Your banner over them is love. You prepare a feast for them in the presence of their enemies. You welcome my grandchildren as guests, anointing their heads with oil. Their cup overflows with blessings. Surely Your goodness and unfailing love will pursue them all the days of their life, and they will live in the house of the LORD forever. Lord God, be the center of my grandchildren's lives, a Mighty One, a Savior Who saves! Rejoice over my grandchildren with joy. Rest in silent satisfaction over them, and in Your love, be silent and make no mention of past sins, or even recall them; exult over my grandchildren with singing. In Jesus' Name, I pray. Amen.

(Jer. 31: 3 TAB; Ps. 37: 23; SS 2: 4; Ps 23; 5–6; Zeph. 3: 17)

Father, as I sit quietly before You praying for my grandchildren, is there any word, Scripture, insight, or particular situation related to this topic of Your delight which concerns my grandchildren that You want to bring to my heart? I surrender my thoughts to You and I commit to pray in obedience to what You reveal.

Word:

Date:

Repentance

Heavenly Father, it is a child's nature to at times to misbehave and rebel against authority. They are too young to realize that rebellion against authority is rebellion against You. There will be times when my adult children will need to apply godly discipline. For what father and mother who love their children do not discipline? I know that You, Lord, discipline those You love, and You punish those You accept as Your children. Since I respect my earthly father who disciplined me, should I not all the more cheerfully submit to the discipline of You, my heavenly Father, and live forever? For my earthly father disciplined me for a few years, doing the best he knew how. But Your discipline is always right and good for me because it means I will share in Your holiness. No discipline is enjoyable while it is happening—it is painful! But afterward there will be a quiet harvest of right living for those who are trained in this way.

I pray, Father, that my grandchildren's response to correction will be a sorrow that leads to true repentance. May they become sorrowful as You intend and so are not harmed. Your Word tells me that sorrow without repentance results in death. May my grandchildren recognize that their parents' reaction to rebellion reflects Your character and leads them to repentance. May their parents demonstrate kindness, tolerance and patience in their parental role. May these parents gently instruct my grandchildren in the hope that You will grant them true repentance leading them to a knowledge of the truth. I pray this in the Name of Your Son. Amen.

(Hebrews 12: 6, 8; 2 Cor. 7: 9; Romans 2: 4; 2 Tim. 2: 25)

Father, as I sit quietly before You praying for my grandchildren, is there any word, Scripture, insight, or particular situation related to discipline which concerns my grandchildren that You want to bring to my heart? I surrender my thoughts to You and I commit to pray in obedience to what You reveal.

Word:

Date:

Serving God

Lord God, for Believers, serving You is the highest privilege. With gratitude for Your unfailing love, my grandchildren will walk after You and serve You with all their minds and hearts and entire beings, keeping Your commandments and Your statutes which You command them today for their good. You they must follow, and You they must revere. They will study Your Word and eat the very words You have spoken, and they will hold fast to You, serving You with their very lives. I pray, in view of all Your mercies, my grandchildren will give their bodies to You. Let them be living and holy sacrifices ~ the kind You will accept. Preserve them from copying the behavior and customs of this world, but transform them into new persons by changing the way they think. Then they will know what You want them to do, and they will know how good and pleasing and perfect Your will is. Serving You includes loving others with brotherly affection as members of one family, giving precedence and showing honor to others. May they never lag in zeal and in earnest endeavor as You set them aglow, burning with the Spirit, serving You. I pray that my grandchildren will do what You require and will not turn aside from following You, but will serve You with all their heart. Keep them from running after vain and worthless things which cannot profit or deliver them, for they are empty and futile. Do not forsake Your people, my grandchildren, for Your great Name's sake, for it has pleased You to make them a people for Yourself. I pray that my grandchildren will know that they have personal knowledge of You. They will understand You; appreciate, heed, and cherish You; they will serve You with a blameless heart and a willing mind. For

You, Lord, search all hearts and minds and understand all the wanderings of their thoughts. If they seek You, they will find You. May my grandchildren serve You with gladness! May they come before Your Presence with singing! May they know that the Lord is God! It is You Who have made them, not they themselves, and they are Yours! They are Your people and the sheep of Your pasture. In Jesus' Name, I pray.

(Deut. 13: 4; Matt 4: 10; Joshua 22: 5; Rom. 12: 1–2; Rom. 12: 10–11; Ex. 23:25; Deut. 10: 12–13; 1 Sam. 12: 20–22; 1 Chron 28:9; Ps.100: 2–3)

Father, as I sit quietly before You praying for my grandchildren, is there any word, Scripture, insight, or particular situation related to serving You which concerns my grandchildren that You want to bring to my heart? I surrender my thoughts to You and I commit to pray in obedience to what You reveal.

Word:

Date:

Surrendered Life

Heavenly Father, I pray that my grandchildren will not have partially surrendered lives ~ Christian in spirit, but secular in practice. I pray that in my grandchildren's lives, Jesus is not only Savior, but Lord. May they not merely add Jesus to their lives as another interest, but surrender their lives to His love and cause. May they not seek the God they want, but the God Who is. May they be so completely preoccupied with Jesus that they hunger for their own lives to reflect His life. I proclaim that Jesus is the Christ, the Son of the living God. May my grandchildren not mistake His identity. May they not think too narrowly of Him. May they release their perceptions of Who You are and Who they want You to be. Enlarge their small thinking and understanding. Your kingdom come in the lives of my grandchildren. Your will be done in their lives, here and now, on earth as it is in heaven. I have begun to understand that to fully surrender means to be so completely dependent upon Christ that obedience brands my behavior. May my grandchildren surrender the temporal kingdom they may build as they grow up, and may You give them the eternal kingdom gained from a surrendered life. You oppose the proud but give grace to the humble. May my grandchildren willingly submit themselves to You. May they resist the devil and he will flee from them. Draw near to them, Lord, as they come near to You. I pray this in Jesus' Name. Amen.

(James 4: 6–8)

Father, as I sit quietly before You praying for my grandchildren, is there any word, Scripture, insight, or particular situation related to this topic which concerns my grandchildren that You want to bring to my heart? I surrender my thoughts to You and I commit to pray in obedience to what You reveal.

Word:

Date:

Teacher - 1

adapted from a Charles Spurgeon devotional

Heavenly Father, there are many who can bring the Scriptures to the mind, but You alone can prepare the mind to receive the Scriptures. You differ from all other teachers; other teachers reach the ear, but You instruct the heart; others deal with the outward letter, but You impart an inward taste for the truth, by which we perceive its savor and spirit. Father, I pray that You will open the understanding of my grandchildren.

My prayer is that my unlearned grandchildren will become ripe scholars in the school of grace when the Lord Jesus unfolds the mysteries of the kingdom to them by His Holy Spirit. Give them a divine anointing by which they are enabled to behold the invisible. They will be blessed if they have had their understanding cleared and strengthened by the Master! How many men of profound learning are ignorant of eternal things. They know the letter of revelation, but its spirit they cannot discern; they have a veil upon their hearts which the eyes of carnal reason cannot penetrate. May that not be the case for my grandchildren. Though they are young and utterly blind; though truth may be to them as beauty in the dark, a thing unnoticed and neglected, I stand upon the promise that they will see!

Without the love of Jesus, they will remain in utter ignorance, for without Your gracious opening of their understanding, they cannot attain to spiritual knowledge any more than an infant can climb the mountain, or an ostrich fly up to the stars. Jesus is the only One by Whom Your truth can be really learned; others may teach them what is to be believed, but Christ alone can show my grandchildren how to believe it. May my grandchildren sit at the feet of Jesus, and by earnest prayer call on His blessed aid that their limited minds may grow brighter, and their feeble understandings may receive heavenly revelation. I pray this in Your Son's Name. Amen.

(Luke 24: 45)

Father, as I sit quietly before You praying for my grandchildren, is there any word, Scripture, insight, or particular situation related to this topic which concerns my grandchildren that You want to bring to my heart? I surrender my thoughts to You and I commit to pray in obedience to what You reveal.

Word:

Date:

Teacher - 2

adapted from a Charles Spurgeon devotional

Heavenly Father, I am grateful that Jesus not only imparts truth to us, He also helps us to accept it. This is the task of any teacher, but mortal teachers can only work from the exterior, trying to clear pupils' minds of the errors which obscure, and trying to present the truth in a clear and convincing manner. Jesus does much more than this; His activity is far more intimate and profound. He is the only Teacher capable of acting directly on the soul, mind, and will of His pupils. I praise You that Jesus will move the souls of my grandchildren to interiorly accept His teachings and to put them into practice.

O Lord Jesus, I ask You to exercise all Your power as Divine Teacher over my grandchildren. May they grow to love Your words of instruction in order to bring forth fruit. After they have listened to You in prayer and made a resolution to put into practice what You have purposed to make them understand, may they not forget it at the opportune moment nor allow themselves to be overcome by habitual frailty. Teach them to retain and deeply penetrate Your truths into their inner being. Help them to recall Your truths so that distractions and useless preoccupations will not stifle them. They will not be like the careless farmer who allows the good grain to be choked out by weeds. In times of difficulty, when they should be carrying out Your instructions, may they learn to turn to You, their Divine Teacher, always present and operating in them by Your grace! May they place themselves at Your feet and implore Your help. How they will profit! I know You are always ready to receive my grandchildren and to increase their faith so that they might see everything in Your light and regard all circumstances according to their value for eternity. You are always eager to kindle in their hearts a more ardent flame of love and to draw them gently to the practice of what You have taught them.

People weary themselves seeking learned teachers; they spend a great deal of money; they take long journeys and make many sacrifices to consult them even for a few brief moments. May my grandchildren know that they always have at hand the Divine Teacher. May they know enough to take advantage of Your teaching. O Jesus, infinite wisdom and knowledge, You do not hesitate to come to my grandchildren to be their Guide and Master. Do not permit them to be so foolish as to forget You. May they always be people who listen to Your Word and continually seek Your light and strength. I pray this in the power of Your Name. Amen.

Father, as I sit quietly before You praying for my grandchildren, is there any word, Scripture, insight, or particular situation related to this topic which concerns my grandchildren that You want to bring to my heart? I surrender my thoughts to You and I commit to pray in obedience to what You reveal.

Word:

Date:

Things Above

Heavenly Father, I pray that as my grandchildren grow, they will set their minds on things above and not on things on the earth. I pray that they will not love the world nor the things of the world, for Your Word says that this demonstrates the love of the Father is not in them. I pray that my grandchildren will not lay up for themselves treasures on earth, where moth and rust destroy and where thieves break in and steal. Help my grandchildren lay up for themselves treasures in heaven, for where this treasure is, so will their hearts be. Whenever they face affliction, help them recognize that it is only for a moment. You allow these tests so that their inner man is renewed day by day as they walk by faith and not by sight. This is a far more exceeding and eternal weight of glory. May my grandchildren not look at the things which are seen, but at the things which are unseen. For the things which are seen are temporary, but the things which are not seen are eternal. You, Father, have reserved for my grandchildren an inheritance that is incorruptible and undefiled and does not fade away. Your grace will appear to my grandchildren. It will teach them to say, "No," to ungodliness and worldly passions, and to live self-controlled, upright, and godly lives in this present age while they wait for that blessed hope of eternal life with Jesus. In gratitude for this gift, I pray. Amen.

(Col. 3: 2; 1 John 2: 15; Matt. 6: 19–21; 2 Cor. 5: 7;
2 Cor. 4: 16–18; 1 Peter 1: 4; Titus 2: 11–12)

Father, as I sit quietly before You praying for my grandchildren, is there any word, Scripture, insight, or particular situation related to this topic which concerns my grandchildren that You want to bring to my heart? I surrender my thoughts to You and I commit to pray in obedience to what You reveal.

Word:

Date:

Waiting

Heavenly Father, I believe that the most important thing I can do for my grandchildren is pray Your very words over them. Hear my prayers and help my grandchildren learn to wait on You, for Your timing is always perfect. In the morning, O LORD, may You hear my grandchildren's voices as they awaken; in the morning stir them to lay their requests before You and wait in expectation. I pray my grandchildren will wait patiently for You; turn to them, O God, and hear their cry. May it be said in that day, "Behold my God upon Whom I have waited and hoped, that He might save me! This is the Lord, I have waited for Him; I will be glad and rejoice in His salvation." May my grandchildren wait in hope for the LORD; You are their help and their shield. May my grandchildren wait for You in their souls. May they put their hope in Your Word. May their souls wait for You more than watchmen wait for the morning. Help them be strong and take heart and wait for the LORD. I pray that their souls will wait only upon You and silently submit to You; for their hope and expectation are from You. May they seize and hold fast and retain without wavering the hope they confess, for He Who promised is reliable and faithful to His Word. May my grandchildren be those who wait for the Lord, for then they will change and renew their strength and power; they will lift their wings and mount up close to God as eagles; they will run and not be weary, they will walk and not faint or become tired. O LORD; You will answer. You long to be gracious to them; You rise to show Your compassion. For the LORD is a God of justice. May my grandchildren be blessed as they wait for You! In Jesus' Name. Amen.

(Ps. 5: 3; Ps. 40: 1; Is. 25: 9; Ps. 33: 20; Ps. 130: 5–6; Ps. 27: 14;
Ps. 62: 5; Heb. 10: 23; Is. 40: 31; Ps. 38: 15)

Father, as I sit quietly before You praying for my grandchildren, is there any word, Scripture, insight, or particular situation related to this topic on waiting which concerns my grandchildren that You want to bring to my heart? I surrender my thoughts to You and I commit to pray in obedience to what You reveal.

Word:

Date:

Prayers for Facing
Daily Challenges

Armor of God

Father, my grandchildren will need Your covering every morning as they awaken. They have a formidable enemy whose purpose is to harm them. I pray that they will be dressed daily in the full armor of God, so that they will be able to stand against the schemes of the devil. Put on them the belt of truth. In ancient wars, the girdle braced and supported the body and held the armor together. So does Your Truth. Your Word is my grandchildren's support on which they can stand. Place on my grandchildren the breastplate of righteousness, a covering which in earlier times had a front and back and fell from the neck to the thighs. This spiritual breastplate is faith and love, integrity and holiness. My grandchildren are the righteousness of God in Christ Jesus. Shoe their feet with the Gospel of peace. Shoes had cleats so the warrior could stand firm. Help my grandchildren plant their feet, stand, and fight. Let them take up the shield of faith, wherewith they will be able to quench all the fiery darts of the wicked. The enemy will send his fiery arrows. They will come suddenly from unexpected quarters. They are meant to torment the soul and set it on fire. Sudden temptations, unbelief, and doubt, thoughts that wound are all weapons formed against my grandchildren. On their head place the helmet of salvation, so they will hold the thoughts, feelings, and purposes of Your heart. May they grab hold of the Sword of the Spirit, an essential part of their armor. This is their offensive weapon ~ Your Word. In the face of all trials, tests, temptations, and tribulation, may they cut to pieces the snare of the enemy by speaking the Word of God. Greater are You Who resides in my grandchildren than he that is in the world. In the Name of

Jesus, may they stand against the wiles of the devil; for they wrestle not against flesh and blood, but against principalities, powers, and rulers of the darkness of this world, and spiritual wickedness in high places. Thank You, Father, for Your powerful armor. May my grandchildren learn to pray at all times ~ on every occasion, in every season ~ in the Spirit, with all manner of prayer and entreaty. To that end, they will keep alert and watch with strong purpose and perseverance, interceding on behalf of all the saints. Their power and ability and sufficiency are from You Who have qualified them as ministers and dispensers of a new covenant of salvation through Christ Jesus. Amen.

(Eph. 6: 10–18; 2 Cor. 5: 21)

Father, as I sit quietly before You praying for my grandchildren, is there any word, Scripture, insight, or particular situation related the armor of God which concerns my grandchildren that You want to bring to my heart? I surrender my thoughts to You and I commit to pray in obedience to what You reveal.

Word:

Date:

Addiction

Heavenly Father, all children come into this world craving to be loved and cared for. You have designed them for relationships with others and especially a relationship with You. Regretfully, some children will be damaged by the neglect or selfishness or abuse of their parents or caretakers. I claim in the power of the Holy Spirit that it will not be so for my grandchildren. May my grandchildren be raised in the nurturing care of their Lord and parents or caretakers.

For those children who have been painfully harmed, behaviors may result which are emotionally driven. Lies spoken by the enemy will create an insatiable void which children might seek to fill with other things such as people, money, food, sex, drugs, alcohol, or pleasure. They will look to other things for gratification to cover their pain. Father, I call on Your Name to deliver these children. Help them find a way to You to receive truth. Delve into their hearts and minds to uncover the lies they believe from early memories which now drive their current behavior. If they believe they are shameful because of painful childhoods and early violations, the shaming lie must be dispelled in the Name of Jesus. Speak to them of Your purifying work done on the Cross. If they carry a feeling of being unprotected because an adult abandoned or violated them, draw near to them, O God, and bring them Your truth that You are ever present. If they believe they are trapped, that their life is never going to get better, that they have no reason to live, You, Lord, speak the truth that You have formed them for Your very own purposes. If they are overwhelmed with fear and dread of the future, keep them from using any substance that will deaden the pain. Intervene, Lord God, and let them know You have promised them hope and a future. I pray for godly counselors, intercessors, mentors, and friends for any child trapped in an addiction. Bring caring ministers alongside to reach out to these precious ones. You, Almighty God, will bring them out of a horrible pit, out of the miry clay; You will set their feet upon a rock, and establish their goings. Deliver them, O Lord, I pray in Your Son's Name. Amen.

(Ps. 34: 18; Jer. 29: 11; Ps. 40: 2)

Father, as I sit quietly before You praying for my grandchildren, is there any word, Scripture, insight, or particular situation related to this topic on addictions which concerns my grandchildren that You want to bring to my heart? I surrender my thoughts to You and I commit to pray in obedience to what You reveal.

Word:

Date:

Built on a Solid Foundation

Lord God, I pray that You will guide my grandchildren so that they will grow and mature in You. I pray that they will be built solidly on the foundation of Jesus. They will grow in Your grace with a conscious sense of Your Presence. May they speak the truth in love, and in all things grow up into Jesus Who is the Head. May they continue to be built up with Your wisdom, favor, truth, love, life, faith, strength, and thankfulness. Just as they receive Christ Jesus as Lord, may they continue to live in Him, rooted and built up in Him, strengthened in the faith as they are taught, overflowing with thankfulness. Like living stones, may my grandchildren be built into a spiritual house for a holy, consecrated priesthood, offering spiritual sacrifices that are pleasing and acceptable to You. In His Name, I pray. Amen.

(Luke2: 52; Eph. 4: 15; Col. 2: 6–7; 1 Peter 2: 5)

Father, as I sit quietly before You praying for my grandchildren, is there any word, Scripture, insight, or particular situation related to this topic which concerns my grandchildren that You want to bring to my heart? I surrender my thoughts to You and I commit to pray in obedience to what You reveal.

Word:

Date:

Child Rearing

Heavenly Father, I believe and confess Your Word which consoles me that You give Your angels charge over my grandchildren to accompany and defend and preserve them in all their ways. You, Lord, are their Refuge and Fortress. On You they can rely and confidently trust. They can depend on You to be their shield, their glory, and the lifter of their heads. In Your wisdom, You also establish protection for my grandchildren through godly parents. From my own experience, I know that it is a serious responsibility to raise children in a loving manner in the fear of the Lord. My prayer is that my own children, as parents, will not provoke their children. When they are tired and emotionally spent, their tendency will be to lash out with wounding words or mete out exaggerated punishment or restrictions. Give them grace, Lord, to hold back and be instructed by Your Spirit. I pray they will lay down the anger of the moment and will not be hard on these children nor cause them to become discouraged nor to feel inferior, nor frustrated. May they never break or wound the spirits of my grandchildren. Help these parents rear their children tenderly in the training, discipline, counsel, and admonition of the Lord. I pray that these parents will train my grandchildren in the way they should go, and when they are old, they will not depart from it. Give their parents kindness and wisdom. Give my grandchildren obedient hearts and a love and respect for their parents. May my grandchildren, from their childhood, have a knowledge of the sacred Scriptures which are able to instruct and give them understanding about salvation which comes through faith in Christ Jesus. I pray these things in Jesus' Name. Amen.

(Ps. 91: 11; Ps. 91: 2; Ps. 3:3; Col. 3: 21; Eph. 6:4; Prov. 22: 6;
2 Tim. 3: 15)

Father, as I sit quietly before You praying for my grandchildren, is there any word, Scripture, insight, or particular situation related to this topic on child rearing which concerns my grandchildren that You want to bring to my heart? I surrender my thoughts to You and I commit to pray in obedience to what You reveal.

Word:

Date:

Confusion and Worry

Heavenly Father, some of my grandchildren are older and already in school, and some are still toddlers. I know that as they mature, they will face things that bring confusion to their minds and souls in these challenging and troubling times. Help them know that Your Word says You are the Author of Peace and not confusion, and that they are to lean on You and Your Word and not their own understanding. They must not rely on their own insight. They must recognize and acknowledge You, Lord God, and You will direct and make their paths straight and plain. Teach them the way they should go. Counsel them with Your eye upon them. Then they will have great peace because they love Your law, and nothing will offend them or make them stumble. Lead them to cast their burdens on You, Lord, releasing the weight of them, and You will sustain them. You will never allow the consistently righteous to be made to slip, fall, or fail. Give them clarity of thought and the assurance of Your Presence. Your Word says that You will judge those who are troublesome and who stir up confusion. I trust You, Lord, to replace all confusion and doubt, and bring my grandchildren spiritual understanding.

Would You keep my grandchildren from worrying. Instead, help them to pray about everything. May they tell You what they need, and thank You for all You have done. If they do this, they will experience Your peace, which is far more wonderful than the human mind can understand. Your peace will guard their hearts and minds as they live in Jesus. I pray that my grandchildren will always remember that You give power to the faint and weary, and to him who has no might You increase strength, causing it to multiply and making it abound. I pray that my grandchildren will know that wherever there is jealousy (envy) and contention (rivalry and selfish ambition), there will also be confusion (unrest, disharmony, rebellion) and all sorts of evil and vile practices. But Your wisdom that comes from heaven is first of all pure. It is also peace loving, gentle at all times, and willing to yield to others. It is full of mercy and good deeds. It shows no partiality and is always sincere. It is wholehearted, straightforward, and impartial; it is free from doubts, from wavering, and from insincerity. For You, God, are not a God of confusion and disorder but a God of peace and order. May this peace be evident in the lives of my grandchildren. In Jesus' Name, I pray. Amen.

(Prov. 3: 5–6; Ps. 32: 8; Ps. 119: 165; Ps. 55: 22;
Gal. 5: 10: Phil. 4: 6–7; Is. 40: 29; James 3: 16–17;
1 Cor. 14: 33)

Father, as I sit quietly before You praying for my grandchildren, is there any word, Scripture, insight, or particular situation related to this topic which concerns my grandchildren that You want to bring to my heart? I surrender my thoughts to You and I commit to pray in obedience to what You reveal.

Word:

Date:

Do Not Fear

O Lord, take my grandchildren's hands so that they will not fear. Lead them through difficult times, letting them know that You are near. My grandchildren will not be dismayed. You will strengthen, help, and uphold them with Your righteous right hand. Father, when my grandchildren are afraid, may they put their confidence in You. Yes, they will trust Your promises. And since they trust You, what more can man do to them? You have not given them a spirit of timidity, but of power and love and sound judgment. Therefore, my grandchildren will not be ashamed of the testimony of their Lord. They have not received a spirit of slavery leading to fear again, but they have received a spirit of adoption as sons and daughters by which they can cry out, "Abba, Father!" I pray that Your truth, God, will be my grandchildren's shield and buckler and that they will not be afraid. I pray that You will give Your angels charge over my grandchildren, to keep them in all their ways. In Jesus' Name. Amen.

(Isaiah 40:31; Ps. 56: 3–5; 2 Tim. 1:7; Rom 8: 15; Ps. 91: 4–5, 11)

Father, as I sit quietly before You praying for my grandchildren, is there any word, Scripture, insight, or particular situation related to fear which concerns my grandchildren that You want to bring to my heart? I surrender my thoughts to You and I commit to pray in obedience to what You reveal.

Word:

Date:

Dress

Heavenly Father, my grandchildren live in a culture that is counter to a life of purity. They are battered on all sides by pressures to succumb to exhibiting their bodies in degrading fashion. I pray that You will strengthen their inner man to stand against this culture's values. The world is full of sin, obeying Satan, the mighty prince of the power of the air. He is the spirit at work in the hearts of those who refuse to obey You. All of us used to live that way, following the passions and desires of our evil nature. We were born with an evil nature, and we were under Your anger just like everyone else. But You, God, are so rich in mercy, and You loved us so very much, that even while we were dead because of our sins, You gave us life when You raised Christ from the dead. My grandchildren live in this world, but they are no longer of this world. It is only by Your special favor that my grandchildren have been saved! For You raised them from the dead along with Christ, and they are seated with Him in the heavenly realms ~ all because they are one with Christ Jesus. Father, forgive my grandchildren for the times they have watched, read, listened, or participated in vile things. Forgive them for wanting to yield to the carnality of this age. May they submit themselves to Jesus, Who loves them and gave Himself up for them, so they might be sanctified in their bodies, behavior, and even dress, having cleansed them by the washing of the water with the Word. May they be presented to You in glorious splendor, without spot or wrinkle, that they might be holy and faultless. The night is almost gone; the day of salvation will soon be here. Keep them from living in darkness. Help them get rid of their evil deeds. May they shed them like dirty clothes. May they clothe themselves with the armor of right living, as those who live in the light. Since You chose them to be the holy people whom You love, clothe them with tenderhearted mercy, kindness, humility, gentleness, and patience. May they buy gold from Jesus ~ gold that has been purified by fire. Then they will be rich and will purchase white garments so they will not be shamed by their nakedness. Make my grandchildren pure before You in dress, thought, and deed. In Jesus' Name, I pray. Amen.

(Eph. 2: 2–6; Eph. 5: 26–27; Rom. 13: 12; Col. 3: 12; Rev. 3: 18)

Father, as I sit quietly before You praying for my grandchildren, is there any word, Scripture, insight, or particular situation related to this topic which concerns my grandchildren that You want to bring to my heart? I surrender my thoughts to You and I commit to pray in obedience to what You reveal.

Word:

Date:

Failure

Thank You that You are the God of redemption! I cannot keep count of the mistakes I have made throughout my life. My grandchildren will also make mistakes, BIG mistakes, but these will give them opportunities to know Your character of mercy. They will fall into self-recrimination when they know their mistakes are their own fault. They will want to hide. Adam and Eve did this in the garden until You asked the first question of the Bible, "Where are you?" Why are you hiding? Each time my grandchildren fail, please send Your Holy Spirit to guide them in examining what went wrong. They will need to learn from their mistakes. When did they shut their ears to Your Voice? When did they stop following Your instruction? When did they start to believe they could go forward without You? Lead them to a solution, Lord, even if it is merely to repent and apologize to others. Thank You for trusting them with the lessons they will draw from their mistakes. You will make all things work for their good because You long to bring redemption and restoration to every crisis. You make all things new.

May they never self-justify. May they admit to their failures without blaming others. Give them favor with those who need to extend forgiveness. Father, keep them from ever believing the lies that they are stupid; they should have done more to prevent the mistake; they deserve rejection; they are bad; everything is out of control; not even You can help them. You are the lifter of their heads. You will rescue them again and again, because the LORD says, "I will rescue those who love Me. I will protect those who trust in My name. When they call on Me, I will answer; I will be with them in trouble. I will rescue them and honor them." Thank You that every mistake is redeemable through the working of Your Holy Spirit. Amen.

(Eph. 4:30; Gen. 3: 9; Rom. 8: 28; Rev. 21: 5; Ps. 3: 3;
Ps. 91: 14–15 NLT)

Father, as I sit quietly before You praying for my grandchildren, is there any word, Scripture, insight, or particular situation related to this topic which concerns my grandchildren that You want to bring to my heart? I surrender my thoughts to You and I commit to pray in obedience to what You reveal.

Word:

Date:

Friendship and Dating

Heavenly Father, how much I appreciate the friends You have brought to my life. They have been authentic and caring fellow pilgrims on my journey of faith. I pray that You will also grant my grandchildren healthy, edifying, satisfying, and wise friendships. The people with whom they choose to spend time will influence their conduct and thinking. Draw my grandchildren to righteous companions. Your Word encourages my grandchildren to be companions of all those who fear, revere, and worship You, and all those who observe and give heed to Your precepts. May they have the character and high calling to follow Your example in expressing their love by a willingness to lay down their own lives for their friends.

In time, these grandchildren may want to date. Keep them from being in a hurry, Lord! Give them opportunities to meet other young people of the opposite gender in order to develop relationships which are true, wholesome, and mutually encouraging. Teach them how to relate well in ways that bring honor to You. Keep them pure with You as the keystone of friendships and dating relationships.

Father, I already ask for your blessing on my grandchildren's future spouses. You, Who are outside of time, have established these relationships for Your glory. I pray that my grandchildren will find the godly life partner that You are preparing for them, even if they have not yet been born. In Your timing, give each of them helpmates who will compliment them in their obedient walk with You. I trust You to develop the character of Jesus in their future mates. Let their walk together with You be an undeniable testimony that You made them for each other. Bless them with Your best. I pray this in Jesus' Name. Amen.

(Ps. 119: 63; John 15: 13; John 15:14; Prov. 12:4; Prov. 31: 10; Ps. 112: 1–2)

Father, as I sit quietly before You praying for my grandchildren, is there any word, Scripture, insight, or particular situation related to this topic which concerns my grandchildren that You want to bring to my heart? I surrender my thoughts to You and I commit to pray in obedience to what You reveal.

Word:

Date:

Healthy Lifestyle

Father, my grandchildren have been created by Your hand. I proclaim that Jesus is Lord over their spirits, souls, and bodies. I praise You because they are fearfully and wonderfully made. Your works are wonderful; how well I know that. I watch them grow and marvel at the perfection of Your work. May each of my grandchildren value their bodies and choose to renew their minds for a healthy lifestyle. May they commit to take care of their bodies. You have given them prudence and wisdom. The simpleton believes every word, but the prudent considers well his steps. Therefore, help them to give thought to their steps. Teach them knowledge and good judgment. May they believe in Your commands, for You give wise counsel about how they should eat and drink, exercise and rest. Your Word teaches that their bodies are temples of the Holy Spirit. Their bodies are for You, Lord. With Your help, teach them to take their everyday, ordinary life ~ their sleeping, eating, going-to-school, walking, and playing ~ and place it before You as an offering. This is their spiritual worship. Help them exercise properly and value their time outdoors glorying in Your creation. Keep them from habits of gluttony, overindulgence, slothfulness, or denying themselves nutrition for vanity's sake. May Jesus be magnified and receive glory and praise in these little bodies and be boldly exalted in their persons. Help them learn ways to live a healthy lifestyle in order to honor You and be available for Your service. In Jesus' Name. Amen.

(Ps. 139: 14; Jer. 29:11; Prov. 14:15; Ps. 119: 66; Rom. 12:1; Phil. 1: 20)

Father, as I sit quietly before You praying for my grandchildren, is there any word, Scripture, insight, or particular situation related to this topic which concerns my grandchildren that You want to bring to my heart? I surrender my thoughts to You and I commit to pray in obedience to what You reveal.

Word:

Date:

Internet Use

Lord, who could have imagined how dramatically our lives would change with technology and the internet? Countless benefits have come, but some aspects of the internet have had terrible consequences for our society. I thank You for the good uses of the internet in my grandchildren's lives, and I beg You for protection from evil intentions of others and the enemy to bring destruction into their homes. Father, there is no filter like the filter of the Holy Spirit. I pray that You would guard my grandchildren from any access to information that would be harmful. Keep their parents ever vigilant to observe what and how their computer is put to use. Thank You that they can have libraries of good literature at their fingertips. They can instantly contact friends and family across the globe. They can download lessons from Christian teachers and compare Bible passages from twenty translations and as many languages in a matter of minutes. Almost any question they have can be answered through the internet encyclopedia.

I also know the deceitful and destructive intention of the enemy to rob, steal, and kill. What You have designed for good, he will counterfeit for evil. First, Lord, give them balance in the amount of time they spend on the computer. Do not let it take precedence over relationships with other people, their family, and time spent with You. The enemy would want to rob them of time. Father, monitor the information they are accessing. You, their heavenly Father, know what wisdom they need. I pray that my grandchildren will seek first Your kingdom and Your righteousness, and all other fruitful knowledge will be given to them as well. May they seek Your counsel first before looking for answers on matters of life from any other source. You, LORD, give wisdom, and from Your mouth comes knowledge and understanding. All good knowledge comes from You, LORD Almighty, wonderful in counsel, and magnificent in wisdom. You will be the sure foundation for our times, a rich store of salvation and wisdom and knowledge; the fear of the LORD is the key to this treasure. I will keep asking You, the God of our Lord Jesus Christ, the glorious Father, to give my grandchildren the Spirit of wisdom and revelation, so that they may know Jesus better. Thank You for the internet and the expansion of shared human knowledge. But keep my grandchildren safe from its abuses. I pray this in the Name of Your Son. Amen.

(Matt. 6: 32–33; 2 Chron. 18: 4; Prov. 2: 6; Is. 8: 29; Is. 33: 6; Eph. 1: 17)

Father, as I sit quietly before You praying for my grandchildren, is there any word, Scripture, insight, or particular situation related to this topic which concerns my grandchildren that You want to bring to my heart? I surrender my thoughts to You and I commit to pray in obedience to what You reveal.

Word:

Date:

Life Valued

Father, Author of Life. You speak and things come into being. You breathe and life begins. You are Creator and You value life. Help my grandchildren know Your heart concerning life. May they never be careless or cavalier when they must stand for life. I believe Your Word which states "in Your book all the days of my life were written before they ever took shape, when as yet there was not one of them," and "Show me, O LORD, my life's end and the number of my days; let me know how fleeting is my life. You have made my days a mere handbreadth; the span of my years is as nothing before You. Each man's life is but a breath." Keep my grandchildren from taking unnecessary risks with their lives. Protect them when they are in cars and boats, when they hike and swim. Help them to consider human life as sacred.

Loving life, I also pray for all my grandchildren that I have lost through premature death or miscarriage. Lord, You knew the number of their days of these precious babies from the moment they were conceived, and I thank You for each one of these lives that I have not known, but are intimately known to You. May they go from strength to strength in Your Kingdom, in Jesus' Name. Amen.

(Ps. 139; Ps. 39: 4–5 NIV; Ps. 84: 7)

Father, as I sit quietly before You praying for my grandchildren, is there any word, Scripture, insight, or particular situation related to this topic which concerns my grandchildren that You want to bring to my heart? I surrender my thoughts to You and I commit to pray in obedience to what You reveal.

Word:

Date:

Living for Eternity

Heavenly Father, before I knew Jesus Christ, this present world was my only frame of reference. When I thought of heaven, it was a distant place where I would eventually go if I were a good person. How ignorant I was of Your promises. Your Word says that You have planted eternity in men's hearts and minds. The Apostle Paul wrote, "If we have hope in Christ only for this life, we are the most miserable people in the world." Ever since I first heard the truth of the Good News, I have been looking forward to the joys of heaven. Father, my prayer is that my grandchildren will have a passion for what endures. May they know that this world is not all that they have nor can expect. Heaven must become their central point of reference for they are created for it, redeemed for it, and on their way to living there eternally. Make living for eternity be the habit of their hearts. When they keep heaven in view, their responses to life will be radically changed. When they keep their minds on heavenly things, life and its faith threatening challenges will diminish in their power. Give them discernment to see not only the world around them, but also a supernatural view of the world to come. If heaven is my grandchildren's hope and the expansion of Your kingdom my grandchildren's calling, then life in this world becomes manageable, for it lasts only for a short while. Their reward is yet to come. Difficult, unanswerable questions and seemingly meaningless injustices can be tolerated if they believe that the King of Glory will settle all things on "the other side" of this transitory life. This is what the LORD says: "Heaven is My throne, and the earth is My footstool. Could you ever build Me a temple as good as that? Could you build a dwelling place for Me?" May my grandchildren know that when this earthly tent they live in is taken down ~ when they die and leave these bodies ~ they will have a home in heaven, an eternal kingdom made by You Yourself and not by human hands. Assurance and peace will be the proof of eternity in their hearts. They will walk through this life with the confidence that they are foreigners and aliens merely passing through on their way to another kingdom for all of eternity. In Jesus' Name. Amen.

(Eccl. 3: 11; 1 Cor. 15:19 NLT; Is. 66: 1 NLT; 2 Cor. 5: 1;
Col. 1: 5; 1 Peter 2: 11)

Father, as I sit quietly before You praying for my grandchildren, is there any word, Scripture, insight, or particular situation related to this topic on eternity which concerns my grandchildren that You want to bring to my heart? I surrender my thoughts to You and I commit to pray in obedience to what You reveal.

Word:

Date:

Loneliness

Heavenly Father, Source of all comfort. If only I could prevent my grandchildren from ever feeling lonely. But loneliness comes to every person, and You have specific purposes for those times. Occasionally my grandchildren will feel abandoned and overlooked. They will sit alone with a heart that beats wildly, their strength failing. When that happens, You will know what they long for, Lord; You will hear their every sigh. The psalmist David often felt deserted. He said, "My loved ones and friends stay away. Even my own family stands at a distance." "I lie awake, lonely as a solitary bird on the roof." "I am scorned by all my enemies and despised by my neighbors ~ even my friends are afraid to come near me. When they see me on the street, they turn the other way." The Apostle Paul also experienced abandonment: "The first time I was brought before the judge, no one was with me. Everyone had abandoned me." Job said, "My close friends abhor me. Those I loved have turned against me." We know that all of Jesus' disciples deserted Him and ran away.

Use these times of loneliness, Lord God, to draw my grandchildren close to You. I pray they will cry out to You in prayer. Keep them from blaming You for a life full of trouble. May they never feel forgotten, cut off from Your care. They are not in a trap with no way of escape. You always provide a way for them. When their eyes are blinded by tears, and they lift their pleading hands for mercy, do not stay away. You are close to the brokenhearted; You rescue those who are crushed in spirit. A broken and repentant heart, O God, You will not despise. You, the high and lofty One who inhabits eternity, the Holy One, says this: "I live in that high and holy place with those whose spirits are contrite and humble. I refresh the humble and give new courage to those with repentant hearts. I will bless those who have humble and contrite hearts, who tremble at My word." Thank You, Father, for drawing near to my grandchildren when they feel lonely.

(Ps. 38: 9–11; Ps. 102: 7; 2 Tim. 4: 16 NLT; Ps. 31: 11 NLT; Mark 14: 50; Job 19:19 NLT; Ps. 88: 1–10; Ps. 34: 18; Ps. 51: 17; Is. 57: 15 NLT; Is. 66: 2)

Father, as I sit quietly before You praying for my grandchildren, is there any word, Scripture, insight, or particular situation related loneliness which concerns my grandchildren that You want to bring to my heart? I surrender my thoughts to You and I commit to pray in obedience to what You reveal.

Word:

Date:

Money and Possessions

Father, my grandchildren will need Your help in resisting the world's allurement for acquiring riches and possessions. Your Word warns that it is impossible to serve both You and money. There will be no choice for my grandchildren. They can serve only one master. May they choose to serve You. The wise King Solomon said that those who love money will never have enough. How absurd to think that wealth brings true happiness!

Their parents will need to model good stewardship and a balanced approach to money. Give them Your wisdom. They must instruct their children that You own and control everything. All the animals of the forest are Yours, and You own the cattle on a thousand hills. You give people the power to become rich. Possessions are gifts, a trust given in proportion to Spirit-given abilities, faithfulness, and an obedience in following Your commands. May these parents be guarded from preoccupation with either extreme of accumulating or denouncing wealth. May they be wise in their financial conduct. May they lend freely, conduct their business fairly, and give generously to those in need. Their good deeds will never be forgotten. You will give them influence and honor.

Keep my grandchildren from wanting to purchase everything their friends have. Remove envy from their hearts. King Solomon wrote, "Then I observed that most people are motivated to success by their envy of their neighbors. But this, too, is meaningless, like chasing the wind." I pray that my grandchildren will be satisfied because they have done what is right. When they awaken, they will be fully satisfied, for they will see You face to face. May they stay away from the love of money; may they be satisfied with what they have. For You have said, "I will never fail you. I will never forsake you." Godliness accompanied with contentment is great and abundant wealth. In Jesus' Name, I pray. Amen.

(Matt. 6: 24; Eccl. 5: 10; Deut. 8: 18; Ps. 50: 10; Ps. 112: 5, 9; Eccl. 4: 4 NLT; Ps. 17: 15; Heb. 13:5 NLT; 1 Tim. 6:6)

Father, as I sit quietly before You praying for my grandchildren, is there any word, Scripture, insight, or particular situation related money and possessions which concerns my grandchildren that You want to bring to my heart? I surrender my thoughts to You and I commit to pray in obedience to what You reveal.

Word:

Date:

Negative Pronouncements

Heavenly Father, You desire that all your children be free of lies embedded in our thinking that cause pain and separation. Even though my grandchildren are young, I know that eventually they will experience some event or some negative pronouncement that will wound them. Something painful will happen and it cannot be erased. But I pray that the understanding they gain from the traumatic or negative experience will not result in a lie planted in their mind. I pray that each time my grandchildren access a painful memory, You will be present in power to replace negative interpretations with the truth. Your Word instructs that negative emotions such as fear, depression, abandonment, hopelessness, worry, anxiety, and powerlessness are all the result of faulty thinking and misbelief. My grandchildren will need Your illumination and Your inner healing. Father, when they feel fearful, they will remember that perfect love casts out fear. When they face abandonment, remind them that You are with them always. When my grandchildren feel shame from some action or some personal attack, may they know Your promise that there is no condemnation for those who live in Christ Jesus. Father, when my grandchildren feel a sense of helplessness, remind them that they can do all things through Christ Who brings them strength. At times they will feel invalidated. You will speak to their hearts that Jesus Who knew no sin became sin on their behalf so that they might become the righteousness of God. When my grandchildren feel powerless, they must remember that Jesus is able to do exceeding abundantly above all that they can ask or think according to the power that works in them ~ the same power that raised Jesus from the dead. When they feel confused and overwhelmed, You will tell them that they have not been given a spirit of fear but of a sound mind.

A wound inflicted by others condemns, taunts, and shames. It has the power to affect the way my grandchildren interpret life and choose relationships. If You do not intervene quickly, Father, the enemy will use these lies as perpetual life themes that replay over and over consciously and unconsciously. Deliver my grandchildren from these negative events by establishing them in light and freeing truth. In the power of Jesus' Name, I pray. Amen.

(1 John 4:18; Matt. 28:20; Rom. 8: 1; Phil. 4: 3; 2 Cor. 5: 21; Eph. 3: 20; 2 Tim. 1: 7)

Father, as I sit quietly before You praying for my grandchildren, is there any word, Scripture, insight, or particular situation related to this topic which concerns my grandchildren that You want to bring to my heart? I surrender my thoughts to You and I commit to pray in obedience to what You reveal.

Word:

Date:

Peer Pressure

In Jesus' Name, I pray that low self-esteem, spirits of rebellion, and ungratefulness will have no hold on my grandchildren. Peer pressure will not cause them to waiver from Your standards of holiness. Guilt, envy, and shame will be cast into the sea, and every plan You have for my grandchildren will be completed. There will be times when they are pressured to follow the lead of others toward unrighteous behavior. You are close to them and will cause their inner man to hesitate and consider what choices are available. They will already be aware that according to Your Word, rebellion is the same sin as witchcraft. Rebellion caused the fall of Satan and has been the dominant and besetting sin of man. May my grandchildren take a stand. Even though they are ridiculed or persecuted, may they resist the temptation to sin. Help them obey those who rule over them, and be subject to the rules that are established for their protection. Those in authority watch out for their souls, as those who must give account. I pray my grandchildren will gird up the loins of their minds, be sober, and rest their hope fully upon the grace that is brought to them at the revelation of Jesus. May they be obedient, not slipping into behaviors that offend You as they did when they were ignorant of Your law. As You Who call them is holy, they are to be holy in all their conduct. Keep them from hurting others, from gossip, from heckling, from teasing, from breaking the law, from taking dangerous risks, from showing off, from using illegal and mind changing substances, from lying, cheating, and stealing. I pray that they will know that You resist the proud, but give grace to the humble. If they will humble themselves under Your mighty hand, You will lift them up in due time. I pray that my grandchildren will not present them-selves to sin, but that they will present themselves to You as being alive from the dead. May they offer the members of their bodies as instruments of righteousness. Sin will not have dominion over them, for they are not under the law, but under grace. May they know that Jesus went through suffering and temptation, and He is able to help them when they are being tempted. In Jesus' Name, I pray. Amen.

(Mark 11:22–24; Phil. 4:19; 1 Sam. 15:23; Heb. 13:17;
1 Peter 1: 13–15; 1 Peter 5:5–6; Rom. 6: 12–14; Heb. 2: 18)

Father, as I sit quietly before You praying for my grandchildren, is there any word, Scripture, insight, or particular situation related to this topic on peer pressure which concerns my grandchildren that You want to bring to my heart? I surrender my thoughts to You and I commit to pray in obedience to what You reveal.

Word:

Date:

Plans

Father, how thankful I am that I can approach Your Throne with boldness. You are worthy to receive glory and honor and power, for You created all things, and by Your will they were created and have their being. My grandchildren will make plans for their lives, just as I made plans for mine. I am grateful that You intervened and led my life in a direction I did not expect. Your Word tells me that a man may make his plans, but it is You Who orders his steps. Before they set their minds on how their future will look, I ask You to give these children a complete understanding of what You want them to do with their lives as they join You and Your work throughout the earth. Make them wise with spiritual wisdom. Then the way they live will always honor and please You. May they roll their works upon You, LORD, and You will make their thoughts agreeable to Your will so their plans are established and will succeed. Please direct their steps and make them sure. Let them know that the plans You have for them are God-sized and they will need Your help. They will need faith to accomplish the assignments You have for them. But if they have faith as small as a mustard seed, they will be able to tell mountains to move from here to there. When You let these children know what You want to do through them, it will be something only You can accomplish. How marvelous that You will choose my grandchildren to join You in these tasks. I believe that the world will come to know You when they see Your nature expressed through my grandchildren. For what my grandchildren do with their lives will reveal what they believe about You. You have planned something amazing, far greater than I or they imagine. May they never grow weary in being faithful to that cause. Your reward awaits faithful servants. No one can sum up all You are able to do through one solitary life, wholly yielded and obedient to Your call. May my grandchildren be open to that divine plan You have ordained for them. In the Name of Jesus, may they submit to every kind of wisdom, understanding, practical insight and prudence which You lavish upon them in accordance with the riches and generosity of Your gracious favor. I pray this in Jesus' Name. Amen.

(Hebrews 10:19; Prov. 16: 9; Matt. 17: 20–21; Heb. 12: 1–3)

Father, as I sit quietly before You praying for my grandchildren, is there any word, Scripture, insight, or particular situation related to this topic which concerns my grandchildren that You want to bring to my heart? I surrender my thoughts to You and I commit to pray in obedience to what You reveal.

Word:

Date:

Protection, Covering Blood

Gracious Father, I pray that my grandchildren will be protected by the covering blood of Jesus. I know that it is Your will not to take them out of the world, but that You will keep and protect them from the evil one. I pray that they will know the power of the blood to defeat all the works of the devil. By that power, would You bind the enemy from interfering with Your perfect will in their lives. These children belong to You and have already defeated and overcome the agents of the antichrist, because He Who lives in my grandchildren is greater and mightier than he who is in the world. I pray that my grandchildren will be strong and that the Word of God will abide in them, and they will overcome the wicked one. Help them to be strong and of good courage all their lives. Keep them from being afraid, or dismayed, for You, the Lord their God, are with them whenever they go. I pray this in Jesus' Name. Amen.

*(John 17: 15; Col. 1: 13–14; 2 Thess. 3: 3; 1 John 2: 14;
1 John 4: 4; Joshua 1:9)*

Word:

Date:

Protection by the Shepherd

Gentle Shepherd, protect my grandchildren from harm. If one should stray, do not lose sight of her, but bring each one back into Your care. Shield them from danger, and give them healthy minds and bodies. For You have indelibly imprinted them on the palm of each of Your hands. You are the Good Shepherd; and You know and recognize Your own, and Your own know and recognize You ~ even as truly as the Father knows You and You also know the Father. You have given Your very own life, laying it down on behalf of Your sheep, my grandchildren. May they always listen to Your voice and heed Your call, and so they will become one flock under one Shepherd. You are the Good Shepherd. The sheep that are Your own hear and are listening to Your voice; and You know them, and they follow You. You give them eternal life, and they shall never lose it or perish throughout the ages. To all eternity they shall never by any means be destroyed. And no one is able to snatch them out of Your hand. The Father, Who has given them to You is greater and mightier than all else; and no one is able to snatch them out of the Father's hand. Thank You for such care. In Your Name, I pray. Amen.

(Is. 49:16; John 10:14–16, 27–29)

Father, as I sit quietly before You praying for my grandchildren, is there any word, Scripture, insight, or particular situation related to this topic which concerns my grandchildren that You want to bring to my heart? I surrender my thoughts to You and I commit to pray in obedience to what You reveal.

Word:

Date:

Proclamations of Protection

I pray for my grandchildren, here on earth, and those who are to come:

My grandchildren's God, Who goes before them, will fight for them. *(Deut. 1:30)*

If my grandchildren will indeed obey Your Voice, and do all that You speak, then You will be an enemy to their enemies and an adversary to their adversaries. *(Exo. 23:22)*

No weapon formed against them will prosper and every tongue which rises against them in judgment, You God, shall condemn. *(Is. 54:17)*

Jesus has given my grandchildren the authority to trample on serpents and scorpions, and over all the power of the enemy, and nothing shall by any means hurt them. *(Luke 10:19)*

If You are for my grandchildren, who can be against them? *(Rom. 8:31)*

You preserve the souls of my grandchildren, and deliver them out of the hand of the wicked. *(Ps. 97:10)*

The Son of God was manifested that He might destroy the works of the devil to harm my grandchildren. *(1 John 3:8)*

They know You have disarmed principalities and powers, and have made a public spectacle of them, triumphing over them in it. *(Col 2: 15)*

My grandchildren are strong, and that the Word of God abides in them and they have overcome the wicked one. *(1 John 2: 14)*

My grandchildren will not give place to the devil. *(Eph. 4: 27)*

You will not take these children out of the world, but You will keep them from the evil one. *(John 17: 15)*

My grandchildren will submit to You and they will resist the devil and he will flee from them. *(James 4: 7)*

My grandchildren will be sober and vigilant because their adversary the devil walks about like a roaring lion, seeking whom he may devour. I pray that my grandchildren will resist him, steadfast in the faith, knowing that the same sufferings are experienced by other Christians in the world. *(1 Peter 5: 8–9)*

You have delivered my grandchildren from the power of darkness and conveyed them into the kingdom of Jesus, in Whom they have redemption through His blood, the forgiveness of sins. *(Col. 1: 13–14)*

In all things they are conquerors through You Who loved them. *(Rom. 8: 37)*

The accuser of my grandchildren, who accuses them before their God day and night, has been cast down. They have overcome him by the blood of the Lamb and by the word of their testimony. *(Rev. 12: 10–11)*

My grandchildren have their senses exercised to discern both good and evil. *(Heb. 5: 14)*

Your Presence will go with my grandchildren forever. *(Exo. 33:14)*

Amen!

Rejection

Father, I know that as my grandchildren enter the world from the safety of their babyhood and loving homes, they will experience rejection. Their hearts will be wounded and they will doubt themselves. I pray that any rejection they experience will not have a lasting effect on their spirits. You revealed to us from Your Word that to appease Sarah's anger, Abraham cast out Hagar and Ishmael. They wandered aimlessly in the desert, Hagar breaking into tears. You saw her misery and met her need. Isaac sent Jacob away. Joseph's brothers cast him into a pit and left him to die. Your prophets were scorned and mocked. Even Your own Son was familiar with rejection. "The Stone rejected by the builders has now become the cornerstone." Father, You promise that You will draw near to the brokenhearted. You rescue those who are crushed in spirit. You heal the brokenhearted, binding up their wounds. You will not crush those who are weak or quench the smallest hope. You will bring full justice to all who have been wronged. You will lift my grandchildren out of the pit of despair, out of the mud and the mire. You will set their feet on solid ground and steady them as they walk along. When my grandchildren feel rejected, may they run to Jesus, Who is the living cornerstone of Your temple. He was rejected by the people, but He is precious to You Who chose Him. Jesus makes my grandchildren accepted. Remind them that although others will reject them, You, Lord, will never forsake them. And surely You are with them always, to the very end of the age. Amen.

(Gen 21: 10; Gen. 28: 5; Gen. 37: 23; Matt. 21: 42 NLT; Ps. 40: 2;
Ps. 34: 18; Is. 42: 3; Ps. 147: 3; 1 Peter 2: 4; Eph. 1: 6;
Matt. 28: 20)

Father, as I sit quietly before You praying for my grandchildren, is
there any word, Scripture, insight, or particular situation related to
rejection which concerns my grandchildren that You want to bring
to my heart? I surrender my thoughts to You and I commit to pray
in obedience to what You reveal.

Word:

Date:

Relocation to New Home

Father, Your Word says that You will work out Your plans for our life, for Your faithful love, O LORD, endures forever. You will not abandon the works of Your hands. You made us. You made from one common origin all nations of men to settle on the face of the earth. And You have definitely determined their allotted periods of time and the fixed boundaries of their habitation and homes. I bring to You my apprehensions concerning my children's move. I ask You to go before this young family to make the crooked places straight in finding and settling into their new home. Give my adult children wisdom to make wise decisions in choosing the movers and packers best qualified to handle their possessions. I know that my children have favor and high esteem in Your sight. Grant them honest dealings with the agencies who will help them become established: utility companies, school systems, banks, the medical community, new employers, neighborhood stores, and everyone involved in their move. Father, I thank You for supplying and preparing the new friends and neighbors that You have appointed to be impacted by the lives of my family. Make my children and grandchildren strong witnesses for you. May their new friends and neighbors minister to my family in return. I pray for other youngsters who will be suitable companions for my grandchildren. Grant that they will be children who enhance my grandchildren's faith walks with You. I trust You to direct my family to a new church home where they can fellowship with like believers, in unity, in freedom of worship and praise, growing in their knowledge of You. Use their unique gifting to bless their new church family and build up that particular Body of Christ.

Father, I commit this move to You, knowing that You provide generously for Your children. I make all these requests known to You with thanksgiving for this new challenge; and the peace that passes all understanding will guard my heart and mind, and those of my children. You will keep us in perfect peace because our minds are stayed on You. Thank You, Father, for blessing this move. Prosper, grow, and strengthen my children, in the Name of Jesus, I pray. Amen.

(Ps. 138: 8; Prov. 3: 4; Acts 17: 25–27 TAB; James 1: 5; Ps. 37: 5)

Father, as I sit quietly before You praying for my grandchildren, is there any word, Scripture, insight, or particular situation related to this topic which concerns my grandchildren that You want to bring to my heart? I surrender my thoughts to You and I commit to pray in obedience to what You reveal.

Word:

Date:

Searching

Lord God, The words that I am about to pray are Your Words taken from Scripture. Please hear them and honor them, I pray. I ask that my grandchildren learn very early that Your thoughts are not their thoughts, neither are Your ways their ways. For as the heavens are higher than the earth, so are Your ways higher than their ways and Your thoughts than my grandchildren's thoughts. I pray that my grandchildren will call to You, God, and that You will answer them and show them great and unsearchable things which they do not know. Make an everlasting covenant with my grandchildren: do not turn away from following them to do them good. Put Your reverential fear in their hearts, so that they will not depart from You. I pray that my grandchildren will know You. Yes, let them be zealous to know the Lord. Your going forth is prepared and certain as the dawn, and You will come to my grandchildren as the heavy rain, as the latter rain that waters the earth. May these grandchildren not be confused in their understanding of You. I pray that my grandchildren will fear not, for with You, there is nothing to fear, for You are with them. May they not look around in terror and be dismayed, for You are their God. You will strengthen and harden them to difficulties. You will help them. You will hold them up and retain them with Your victorious right hand of rightness and justice. I pray that my grandchildren will hold fast the confession of their hope without wavering, for You God, Who promised are faithful. May they search for Wisdom as they would for lost silver and hidden treasures, then they will understand the reverent and worshipful fear of the Lord and find the knowledge of our omniscient God. In Jesus' Name, I pray. Amen.

(Is. 55: 8–9; Jer. 33: 3; Jer. 32: 40; Hosea 6:3; Is. 41: 10;
Heb. 10: 23; Prov. 2:4)

Father, as I sit quietly before You praying for my grandchildren, is there any word, Scripture, insight, or particular situation related to this topic which concerns my grandchildren that You want to bring to my heart? I surrender my thoughts to You and I commit to pray in obedience to what You reveal.

Word:

Date:

Sexuality

Father, this is a topic that makes a grandparent uncomfortable in praying for grandchildren. However, I cannot put my head in the sand, because society is saturated with sexuality in films, clothing, magazines, music, television, and advertisements that my grandchildren will see and hear, and they need my prayers. I grieve at their loss of innocence, and I pray that their exposure will be limited. I will need Your wisdom in supporting the parents and adults who will instruct these children concerning their own sexuality and the sanctity of intimacy in the context of marriage. Your Word affirms our sexuality. You made us male and female. You have told us that we are fearfully and wonderfully made. Everything You have created is good including all the parts of our bodies. Originally, with Adam and Eve, no guilt was attached to the physical act between a man and his wife. In fact, the Scriptures celebrate sexuality as a profound form of communicating love between a man and a woman. Adam *knew* Eve. Elkanah *knew* Hannah his wife. In the Song of Songs, the lover describes his joy in love-making. Christ used marriage to describe His relationship between Himself and His Church. Sexual intimacy in the right context is wonderful and beautiful. I pray that my grandchildren will eventually, in Your appointed time, delight in a life mate to the fullest. But I do not want this relationship to happen outside of a lifelong commitment of marriage, Lord. I pray that they will be kept from responding to a physical desire in acts that dishonor their relationship to You. Their peers will pressure them to experiment with their sexuality. They may be confused by gender identification issues. Promiscuity may even be the norm of their classmates. But instruct them through Your Word that sexual intimacy outside of marriage is forbidden. You warn that You will judge all sin, including immorality. Keep my grandchildren from being hurt in this area, Father. Empower them to keep to Your laws and live under Your blessing. Strengthen them in their inner man to withstand the temptations that will come their way. Rescue my grandchildren from the idolatry of pleasure. May they submit their bodies to You and keep themselves pure until they are united to a partner in sacred marriage. Amen.

(Gen. 1: 27; Ps. 139: 14; 1 Sam. 1: 19; SS 1: 2; Mark 7: 21; 1 Thess. 4: 3–8)

Father, as I sit quietly before You praying for my grandchildren, is there any word, Scripture, insight, or particular situation related to this topic which concerns my grandchildren that You want to bring to my heart? I surrender my thoughts to You and I commit to pray in obedience to what You reveal.

Word:

Date:

Shut In - a Safe Haven

Adapted from a Charles Spurgeon meditation

"The Lord shut him in." Genesis 7:16 NIV

"These are the words of the Holy One, the True One, He Who has the key of David, Who opens and no one shall shut. Who shuts and no one shall open: I know your works and what you are doing. See! I have set before you a door wide open which no one is able to shut." Rev. 3: 7–8 NIV

"And the key of the house of David I will lay upon His shoulder; he shall open and no one shall shut, he shall shut and no one shall open." Is. 22: 22 TAB

Heavenly Father, I know from Your Word that Noah was shut in away from all the world by Your hand of divine love. You closed the door of the ark to protect him from the impending flood. Your door stands between my grandchildren and the world which lies in the hand of the evil one. My grandchildren are not of the world even as our Lord Jesus was not of the world.

Lord, keep my grandchildren from entering into the sin, the gaiety, the pursuits of the world. Keep my grandchildren from playing in the streets of vanity with the children of darkness. You, Heavenly Father, have shut them in. Noah was shut in with his God. "Come into the ark," was Your invitation, by which You clearly showed that You Yourself intended to dwell in the ark with Your servant and his family.

I believe that all the chosen dwell in You and You in them. They are blessed because they are enclosed in the same shelter which contains the triune God, Father, Son, and Holy Spirit. May my grandchildren never be inattentive to that gracious call, "Come, My people, enter into My chambers, and shut My doors about You."

Noah was so shut in that no evil could reach him. Floods lifted him skyward, and winds wafted him on his way. Outside of the ark all was destruction, but inside all was rest and peace.

Without Christ my grandchildren will perish, but in Christ Jesus there is perfect safety. Noah was so shut in that he did not even desire to come out, and my grandchildren who are in Christ Jesus are in Him forever. They will never go out again, for eternal faithfulness has shut them in, and infernal malice cannot drag them out.

The Prince of the house of David shuts and no man opens. In the last days, as Master of the house, He will rise up and shut the door, and it will be of no use for unbelievers to knock, and cry, "Lord, Lord open up for us," for that same door which shuts in the wise virgins will shut out the foolish forever. Lord, keep each of my grandchildren from indulging in the things that feed the flesh. Make it the profound desire of their hearts to unite themselves to You in order to live Your life alone. You offer Your covering to them, my grandchildren, and I ask that You help them to embrace it with all their hearts. Lord, shut in my grandchildren into the life of the Spirit, by Your grace. Amen.

Father, as I sit quietly before You praying for my grandchildren, is there any word, Scripture, insight, or particular situation related to this topic which concerns my grandchildren that You want to bring to my heart? I surrender my thoughts to You and I commit to pray in obedience to what You reveal.

Word:

Date:

Sibling Rivalry

Father, Your Word tells the stories of sibling relationships falling apart through rivalry and jealousy, selfishness and ambition: Cain and Abel; Joseph and his older brothers; David and his older brothers; Abimelech and his half brothers; Absalom and Amnon; Jehoram and his brothers; Moses, Aaron, and Miriam. There was no genuine love and caring between these brothers and sisters. How poor was their testimony. My desire is that my grandchildren will be raised in such a loving fashion that they cherish their brothers and sisters and put down all thoughts of competition and envy. I pray that my adult children will establish their homes on Christ. May they boldly proclaim, "As for me and my family, I will serve the LORD." Then, the foundation of their homes will be solid, built on the Rock. When the rain falls and the floods come and the winds blow and beat against that house, their homes will not fall. Even a child is known by his actions, by whether his conduct is pure and right. May my grandchildren follow the example of Andrew who loved his brother Peter. When Andrew heard Jesus, he dropped everything and followed Him. Your Word reveals that the first thing Andrew did was find his brother, Simon Peter, and tell him, "I have found the Messiah" (which means the Christ). Then Andrew brought Simon to meet Jesus. As my grandchildren grow in their love for their Savior, may they lovingly introduce Him to their brothers and sisters. May their concern be for the welfare of their siblings. May they love each other, protect each other, and want the best for each other. May my grandchildren be like Timothy who from infancy knew the Holy Scriptures which were able to make him wise for salvation through faith in Jesus Christ. Amen.

(Gen. 4, Judges 9; 2 Samuel 13; 2 Chron 21: 4; Num. 12: 1;
Joshua 24: 15; Matt. 7: 25; Prov. 20: 11 NIV;
John 1: 39–42; 2 Tim. 3: 15)

Father, as I sit quietly before You praying for my grandchildren, is there any word, Scripture, insight, or particular situation related to this topic which concerns my grandchildren that You want to bring to my heart? I surrender my thoughts to You and I commit to pray in obedience to what You reveal.

Word:

Date:

Sickness - 1

Heavenly Father, My grandchild is sick and suffering. You, Beloved Physician can heal him; and whatever may be his state at this moment, in prayer, I have hope in Jesus that You will be able to heal him of his sins. I can have hope for each, for all, when I remember the healing power of my Lord; and on their own account, however severe their struggles with sins and sickness, I can yet rejoice! You still dispense Your grace, and work wonders among the sons of men. I praise You, this day, as I remember how You won this child's right to be healed. It was by taking upon Yourself his sicknesses. "By His stripes we are healed."

I pray for the physical, emotional, and spiritual healing of my grandchild. Father, I pray that You will not only heal his little physical body, but that You will speak Your Word over his life. For Your Word is alive and full of living power. It is sharper than any two-edged sword, penetrating into their innermost thoughts and desires. It is the dividing line of the soul and the spirit. The Spirit cuts to the deepest parts of his nature, exposing and sifting and analyzing and judging the very thoughts and purposes of his heart. It exposes him for whom he really is.

Your Word goes out from Your mouth: It will not return to You empty, but will accomplish what You desire and achieve, the purpose for which You sent it. Father, speak Your Word over the life of my grandchild today. May this powerful, wonderful Word bring healing and transformation to this beloved one. Through the authority of Jesus I pray, "Heal him and he will be healed. Save my grandchild and he will be saved. For You are the One I praise." May my grandchild worship You, Lord, and Your blessing will be on his food and water. You will take sickness away from him. I pray this in Your Son's Name. Amen.

(Isaiah 53: 5; 1 Peter 2: 24; Hebrews 4: 12; Is. 55: 11; Jer 17: 14; Ex. 23: 25)

Father, as I sit quietly before You praying for my grandchildren, is there any word, Scripture, insight, or particular situation related to illness and affliction which concerns my grandchildren that You want to bring to my heart? I surrender my thoughts to You and I commit to pray in obedience to what You reveal.

Word:

Date:

Sickness - 2

Father, once again I call out to You as Jehovah Rophe, God my Healer. How many times I have cried out to You. And in Your faithfulness You have healed me and preserved my life. I thank You that You have brought good news to my family so many times. You have healed aches and pains, restored vision, lessened the aching in our backs, and have provided just the right treatment when we have visited our physicians. I express my thanksgiving and adoration. I know Father that You never slumber or sleep, that You never have Your fill of my requests, and that it is Your pleasure to bring good things to Your children. Today I ask that You restore my grandchild to health. The heat of fever, or the shivering of flu; the terror of cancer, or the rage of madness; the filth of leprosy, or the darkness of blindness ~ all knew the power of Your word, and fled at Your command. In every corner of the battlefield, You were triumphant over evil, and received the praise of delivered captives.

It is even so this day. You, my beloved Physician can heal my grandchild; and whatever may be the state of others whom I remember at this moment in prayer, I have hope in Jesus that You will be able to heal them of their sins. My children, my friends, my parents, I can have hope for each, for all, when I remember the healing power of my Lord; and on my own account, however severe my struggles with sins and sickness, I can yet rejoice! You still dispense Your grace, and work wonders among the sons of men. In Jesus' Name, Amen.

(Jer. 30: 17; Ps. 86: 10)

Father, as I sit quietly before You praying for my grandchildren, is there any word, Scripture, insight, or particular situation related to illness and affliction which concerns my grandchildren that You want to bring to my heart? I surrender my thoughts to You and I commit to pray in obedience to what You reveal.

Word:

Date:

Sleep

Heavenly Father, I pray that my grandchildren will have restful, restorative sleep each nap and each night. Thank You for Your angels that encamp around those who fear You; You deliver my grandchildren and keep them safe. The angels excel in strength, do Your bidding, and heed the voice of Your Word. You give Your angels charge over my grandchildren, to keep them in all their ways. I ask You to bring every thought, every imagination, and every dream into the captivity and obedience of Jesus Christ. Father, I thank You that as my grandchildren sleep, their hearts counsel them and reveal to them Your purposes and Your plans. Thank You for sweet sleep, for You promise Your beloved sweet sleep. Therefore my grandchildren's hearts are glad and their spirits rejoice. Their bodies and souls rest and confidently dwell in safety. They will lie down and sleep in peace, for You alone, O LORD, make them dwell in safety. My grandchildren lie down and sleep; they awaken again, because You, the LORD sustain them. As Your Prophet Jeremiah spoke, may they say each morning, "My sleep has been pleasant to me." Indeed, You will watch over my grandchildren - You neither slumber nor sleep. In the Name of Jesus, I pray. Amen.

(Ps. 34: 7; Ps. 103: 20; Ps. 91: 11; 2 Cor. 10: 5; Prov. 3: 24;
Ps. 4:8; Ps. 3: 5; Jer. 31: 26; Ps. 121: 4)

Father, as I sit quietly before You praying for my grandchildren, is there any word, Scripture, insight, or particular situation related to sleep which concerns my grandchildren that You want to bring to my heart? I surrender my thoughts to You and I commit to pray in obedience to what You reveal.

Word:

Date:

Struggles

Lord, protect my grandchildren's hearts from scars caused by the trials and struggles of this life. Thank You that they do not have to become negative, bitter, or pessimistic as a result of circumstances around them, because they have hope and abundant life in You. I know that my grandchildren will be hard-pressed on every side, troubled and oppressed in every way, but they will not be cramped or crushed. They will suffer embarrassments and be perplexed and unable to find a way out, but they will not be driven to despair; because they belong to You. They will be pursued and persecuted, but they will not be deserted to stand alone. They may be struck down to the ground, but they will never be destroyed. Help them to fix their eyes not on what is seen, but on what is unseen, for it is eternal. Protect them from the enemy who speaks lies to their minds. Show them the truth of their adversity, that You are ever Present with them. You will never leave them nor forsake them. In Jesus' Name. Amen.

(2 Cor. 4: 8–9, 16–18)

Father, as I sit quietly before You praying for my grandchildren, is there any word, Scripture, insight, or particular situation related to this topic which concerns my grandchildren that You want to bring to my heart? I surrender my thoughts to You and I commit to pray in obedience to what You reveal.

Word:

Date:

Temptation - 1

Heavenly Father, Your Word says that You know how to deliver my grandchildren that I so love from the temptations that they encounter. You will now and forevermore deliver these grandchildren. The temptations that come into their lives are no different from what others experience. You are faithful. You will keep the temptation from becoming so strong that they cannot stand up against it. When they are tempted, You will show them a way out so that they will not give in to it. Sin will no longer exert dominion over them, since now they are not under the law as slaves. They are under grace as subjects of Your favor and mercy. May Your Word be hidden in their hearts so that they might not sin against You. I pray that my grandchildren will confess and forsake their sins, for then they will obtain mercy. I pray that my grandchildren will not say when they are tempted, "I am tempted from God"; for You are incapable of being tempted by what is evil and You tempt no one. They are tempted when they are drawn away, enticed and baited by their own evil desires, lust, and passions. Then the evil desire, when it has been conceived, gives birth to sin, and sin, when it is fully matured, brings forth death. I pray my grandchildren will not be misled or deceived. I pray my grandchildren will be sober of mind, vigilant, and cautious at all times; for our enemy, the devil, roams around like a lion, roaring in fierce hunger, seeking someone to seize upon and devour. I pray they will withstand him. Help them stand firm in their faith against the devil's onslaught ~ rooted, established, strong, immovable, and determined, knowing that the same identical sufferings are appointed to the whole body of Christians throughout the world. Now to You ~ the One Who is able to keep my grandchildren without stumbling or slipping or falling, presenting them blameless and faultless before the presence of Your glory in triumphant joy and exultation ~ to You be praise! Amen.

(2 Pet 2: 9; 1 Cor. 10: 13; Rom 6: 14; Ps. 119: 11; Prov. 28: 13; James 1: 13–15; 1 Peter 5: 8–9; Jude 1: 24)

Father, as I sit quietly before You praying for my grandchildren, is there any word, Scripture, insight, or particular situation related temptation which concerns my grandchildren that You want to bring to my heart? I surrender my thoughts to You and I commit to pray in obedience to what You reveal.

Word:

Date:

Temptation - 2

Adapted from a Charles Spurgeon Meditation

Most Holy Father, I pray that my grandchildren will not be tempted, but will be delivered from evil. I pray that my grandchildren will earnestly avoid temptation and seek to walk guardedly in the path of obedience, that they will never tempt the devil to tempt them. May they never enter the thicket in search of the lion.

From my vantage point in life, I know that they might dearly pay for such presumption. The lion may cross their path or leap upon them from the thicket, but may they have nothing to do with hunting him. The person that meets with him, even though he wins the day, will find it a terrible struggle. I pray my grandchildren may be spared the encounter. Our Savior Jesus, Who had experience of what temptation meant, earnestly admonished His disciples, "Pray that you enter not into temptation."

But do as they will, my grandchildren will be tempted; hence the prayer "deliver them from evil." You had one Son without sin; but You have no son without temptation. The natural man is born to trouble as the sparks fly upwards, and the Christian child is born to temptation just as certainly.

Father, may my grandchildren always be on their watch against Satan, because, like a thief, he gives no intimation of his approach. Believers who have had experience of the ways of Satan know that there are certain seasons when he will most probably make an attack, just as at certain seasons bleak winds may be expected; thus the Christian is put on a double guard by fear of danger, and the danger is averted by preparing to meet it. Prevention is better than cure. It is better to be so well armed that the devil will not attack, than to endure the perils of the fight, even though one comes off a conqueror. I pray that my grandchildren will not be tempted, and next, I pray that if temptation is permitted, my grandchildren may be delivered from the evil one. In Jesus' Name. Amen.

(Luke 11:4)

Father, as I sit quietly before You praying for my grandchildren, is there any word, Scripture, insight, or particular situation related to this topic on temptation which concerns my grandchildren that You want to bring to my heart? I surrender my thoughts to You and I commit to pray in obedience to what You reveal.

Word:

Date:

Warfare

Heavenly Father, my grandchildren's enemy is Satan. He wants to destroy each one of them who are now alive on earth and my promised grandchildren to come in the future. Lord, as my grandchildren grow, I know that it will be necessary for them to know the enemy of their souls and how to resist him victoriously. As they learn Your principles of living righteously, will You keep Satan from getting the advantage over them, for they will not be innocent of his wiles and intentions. I pray that they will humbly submit to You and resist the devil, thereby defeating him. According to Your Word, when they stand, he will flee from them. May they discern the evil one's tactics and not entertain his lies in their thoughts nor be entrapped by his snares. I pray that my grandchildren will receive Your strength and resurrection power for every spiritual battle. I pray that You, God, will open my grandchildren's eyes, in order to turn them from darkness to light, and from the power of Satan to You, that they may receive forgiveness of sins and an inheritance among those who are sanctified by faith in Jesus Christ. I pray that You will preserve their souls and deliver them out of the hand of the wicked. I pray that my grandchildren will always know that You have disarmed principalities and powers, and have made a public spectacle of them, triumphing over them. I pray that the angel of the Lord encamps around my grandchildren who fear You, and delivers them. I pray that Your Presence will go with my grandchildren forever. In Jesus' Name. Amen.

(2 Cor. 2: 11; James 4: 7; Eph. 6:10; Acts 26: 18; Ps. 97: 10;
Col. 2:15; Ex. 33: 14)

Father, as I sit quietly before You praying for my grandchildren, is there any word, Scripture, insight, or particular situation related to this topic on temptation which concerns my grandchildren that You want to bring to my heart? I surrender my thoughts to You and I commit to pray in obedience to what You reveal.

Word:

Date:

Prayer Requests from
Parents or Grandchildren

_____

_____

_____

_____

_____

_____

_____

_____

_____

_____

_____

_____

_____

Notes

_____

_____

_____

_____

_____

_____

_____

_____

_____

_____

_____

_____

_____

_____

Special Dates or Occasions
to be Remembered

_____

_____

_____

_____

_____

_____

_____

_____

_____

_____

_____

_____

_____

Anniversaries

_____

_____

_____

_____

_____

_____

_____

_____

_____

_____

_____

_____

Birthdays

_____

_____

_____

_____

_____

_____

_____

_____

_____

_____

_____

_____

School Events

Recitals

_____

_____

_____

_____

_____

_____

_____

_____

_____

_____

_____

_____

_____